how to find the
childcare
your child will love

georgina walsh

foulsham
LONDON • NEW YORK • TORONTO • SYDNEY

foulsham

The Publishing ... Bennetts Close, Cippenham, Slough,
Berkshire, S... 1 5AP, England

Foulsham book... ... be found in all good bookshops and direct from
foulsham.com

ISBN: 978-0-57...

Copyright © 20...8 ... na Walsh

Cover photograph © ...

A CIP record for this book is available from the British Library

The moral right of the author has been asserted

While every effort has been made to ensure the accuracy of all the
information contained within this book, neither the author nor the
publisher can be liable for any errors. In particular, since laws and
entitlements change frequently, it is vital that each individual checks
relevant details for themselves.

The web addresses included in this book were all correct at the time
of publication but may change over time. We hope that websites
referred to in the book will be helpful, but by providing the address,
we are not making a recommendation.

For ease of reading and because this is usually the case, childcarers
are referred to as 'she' in this book. There are, of course, plenty of
male childcarers too.

Printed in Great Britain by Creative Print and Design (Wales), Ebbw Vale

Contents

Introduction

Never has the issue of childcare been more emotive. With the press full of negative stories about nurseries on the one hand, and the potential eye-watering cost of a good nanny on the other, it is hard to know where to turn.

Many women return to work while their children are still young and the Government is striving to increase the number who do so. Whether you are working full time, part time or are simply in need of some extra help or a good nursery school, this step-by-step guide will help you work your way through the childcare maze. It will help you to find the right solution to suit your child and give you the peace of mind that your child is happy and safe.

In addition, this book is unique in offering a carefully developed and tested parenting questionnaire to help you define your style of parenting. Specific advice on how to manage each type of childcare is then given according to your style. The book also includes developmental and safety advice and additional suggestions from the experience of other parents.

Finding what is best for you

When it comes to childcare, everyone's family is different and has different circumstances and needs, and these change from one year to the next. Just because something works for your best friend doesn't necessarily mean it will work for you; you need to find what is right for you and your family. That is the principle behind this book, which covers every aspect of choosing childcare:

- Individual chapters dedicated to each type of childcare with simple tables and guides to make deciding what is right for you as easy as possible.
- Questions to ask each type of childcare to help you find the right one for you.
- Advice for parents who have children with special needs.

- Tips for settling your child in with your chosen childcare and for working well with the provider to ensure a lasting and happy childcare solution.
- Safety and developmental advice to help you and your childcare work at making sure your child is safe, happy and thriving.
- A guide to your changing needs to help you make the right childcare decisions over the years.
- A chapter to help you look at your own needs and feelings towards both parenting and childcare.

The thoughts of other parents and childcarers

This book is full of quotes from parents who have been there themselves, so they know just how you are feeling and what you are worried about.

> *'With so many childcare options out there and so many scare stories in the press, how do I go about finding the right childcare?'*

There are also quotes from childcare professionals, which give you the benefit of their broad-ranging experience.

The difference between getting it right or wrong

Making the wrong childcare decision can make life harder and more fraught, rather than easier. Taking the time to get it right and keep it on track can make a huge difference to your children and your family as a whole. The right childcare will, most importantly, nurture your children when you can't be there to do it yourself. However, it can also change your life, allowing you to do what you need to do, when you need to do it. So, let's get that nurturing and the changes to your life underway!

> *'When you have the right childcare, you can be two people at the same time: a mother and the other you.'*

A quick overview of the options

This simple table gives you a quick overview of the childcare options that are considered in more detail in later chapters. Once you have thought carefully about your family's needs, you may be able to eliminate some options using this chart, or you may like to refer back to this chart while you are going through the decision-making process.

Out-of-home childcare

	Hours	Cost	Age of child	Govt inspected	Full- or part-time	Early years funding for 3 years+	Finan-cial help from Govt
Day nursery	7.30am–6pm	From £150 per week	0–4 years	Yes	Either	Yes	Yes
Crèche	Varies	£2.50–£5 per hour	Any	Yes	Part-time	Not usually	Not usually
Nursery school	9am–3.30pm	Varies	2–4 years	Yes	Either (term-time only)	Yes	Yes
Pre-school	am or pm sessions	£3–£8 per session	2–4 years	Yes	Usually part-time (term-time only)	Yes	Yes
Child-minder	Often 8am–6pm	£2.50–£6 per hour	0–12 years	Yes	Either	Yes	Yes
Out-of-school care	Varies	From £2.50 per hour	3–14 years	Yes	Part-time (some term-time only)	No	Yes

In-home childcare

	Hours	Cost	Age of child	Govt inspected	Full- or part-time	Early years funding for 3 years+	Finan-cial help from Govt
Friend or relative	As needed	By agree-ment	Any	No	Either	No	No
Nanny	Up to 11 hours a day	From £230 per week	Any	Not usually	Either	No	If regis-tered
Maternity nurse	24 hours	From £600 per week	0–6 months	No	Full-time	No	No
Au pair	Usually 5 hours a day	£60–£80 per week	Any	No	Part-time	No	No
Mother's help	Up to 11 hours a day	From £130 per week	Any	No	Either	No	No

Part 1

You, Your Children and Your Childcare

CHAPTER 1

All About You

Motherhood changes your life – believe it! You may have heard this many times before, but you will never appreciate how true it is until you are in the thick of it.

Your children are little miracles, and watching them grow and learn is a wonderful and unique experience. Being a parent subjects you to a vast range of emotions – love, worry, guilt, pride and anger to name but a few. It is a never-ending rollercoaster that can switch from one emotion to another with breathtaking speed. But whatever you are feeling, be it good or bad, rest assured that you are not alone. Someone, somewhere will be feeling the same.

This chapter looks at the following topics:

- Some of the practicalities and responsibilities of parenthood.
- The emotions parenthood brings, including those associated with using childcare.
- Your own attitude to parenting and childcare.

So, what is parenthood *really* like?

Knowing what to expect will help you to enjoy parenthood more. If you are reading this as a pregnant mum-to-be you may be feeling rather apprehensive. Not only do you have the wide-eyed hospital dash and arrival of your little bundle to contend with, you then have to master caring for a newborn … before you even venture into the complex area of childcare.

Entering the realm of parenthood brings many positive emotions, often in very intense forms. Everyone is different but here are some of the feelings you may well encounter:

- Total **unconditional love** for your child.
- **Awe** at the person you have created.
- A sense of **being an integral part** of the cycle of life.
- **Bursting pride** in their achievements, from that first smile ...
- **A sense of perspective** – other things can wait as nothing is as important as your child telling you about their first day at school.
- **Immense joy** and **lots of fun** plus a sense of tapping into your own childhood.
- A sense of **doing it right**, building a good person with good values.

The first few years of your child's life are such an exciting time. There are so many highs involved in shaping a new human being – what an amazing thing to be doing! As well as the immense enjoyment children bring, they also increase your responsibilities. But what exactly do people mean when they talk about the responsibilities of parenthood?

'Now you have responsibilities ...'

Looking at the needs that all humans have can help you to understand your responsibilities to your children. Psychologists divide human needs into five simple levels, known as Maslow's Hierarchy of Needs. You should ensure that your child has all of these needs fulfilled.

1 Physiological (or basic) needs: These are the basic needs that need to be met in order for children to survive: food, water, warmth and so on.
2 Need for safety: Children need to be kept out of harm's way and also need to feel safe.
3 Need for love, affection and to belong: Children need to feel loved and to feel they belong within their family or group.
4 Need for esteem: For children to grow into well-rounded human beings, they must have self-esteem, and for this to grow, they must feel valued and respected.
5 Need for self-actualisation: This can be described as doing what you were 'born to do'. By ensuring all your children's other needs are met, you give them the freedom to concentrate on realising their full potential.

You will often fulfil these responsibilities without thinking, but it helps to be aware of what children need in order to maximise their potential. If you have a premier league footballer or the next Picasso gurgling in the cot next to you, you will probably want to do all you can to help them get there. Hopefully, much of the time looking after your child and living up to your responsibilities will seem relatively easy, fun and carefree. However, you do need to know that the arrival of children will change life as you knew it.

'It will never be the same again ...'

This statement is always delivered with a knowing look – but what do people mean? Many, many things change with being a parent, most for the better, but here are four things you may well need to make room for:

- **Tiredness:** This seeps into every corner of your life.
- **More to do:** Your children are totally dependent on you. As well as running your own life you are now responsible for another one, two, three lives or more ... With more to do you have less time for sleep and getting your own things done, so tiredness and frustration can build up.
- **Timekeeping:** Even if you are not a routine-oriented person, having a child makes you look at your watch more. How long since the baby was last fed? How long has the baby been asleep? Additionally, once you start using childcare your life is ruled by pick-up or handover times.
- **Lack of freedom and flexibility:** Wave these concepts goodbye for a while! With young children dependent on you and so much to do, you simply do not have the freedom you used to enjoy. Hang on to as much as you can with your first child, but if you have a second, don't try to fight it too much! The sting in the tail is that on some occasions when you do get some freedom, you may be too tired to enjoy it ...

Before you start panicking and hyperventilating, remember that forewarned is forearmed. With realistic expectations, good organisation – and good childcare – it is possible to minimise some of the more adverse effects of parenthood, leaving more room for the good bits. However, you do also need to be prepared for the emotional downs as well as the ups that this parenting rollercoaster can bring.

Same day, different emotions

While some people take to motherhood like ducks to water, others will admit to struggling at times. Here are some feelings that parents may encounter on the not-so-good days:

- **Worry:** There can be a lot to worry about: safety, developmental issues, feeding issues, your parenting skills ...
- **Frustration:** That your child will not do what you want.

- **Sheer frustration:** That despite all your efforts, your child still won't do what you want.
- **Loneliness:** You can be in a house full of children but feel it is you against the world.
- **Mundane boredom:** The same chores need to be done day in, day out and not everyone finds the conversation of a 2-year-old that stimulating.

> *'It is the same hell, different day. It can be tedious and dull. It wears you down.'*

- **Disappointment in yourself:** That you have lost your temper.
- **Feeling trapped:** You can't just walk out of the door. Any freedom has to be meticulously planned and there is invariably a deadline when you have to be back on duty again.

> *'It is the little things I miss, like being able to go to the bathroom on my own.'*

Mixed with any of these emotions you may also feel resentment and guilt. Resentment of your child, your partner or your situation; guilt about having these negative feelings. You may find yourself thinking: 'How can I resent my own children? Surely no one else would have such thoughts.' Of course, the pendulum will very soon swing back and you will be thinking how incredibly sweet and wonderful they are – hey ho, welcome to parenthood!

The big G ... guilt if you do, guilt if you don't

Like tiredness, guilt can tend to seep into every aspect of your life as a parent. Even if you feel you are doing your very best for your child, it can still track you down.

You may feel guilt that you should be going out to work or, conversely, guilt that you should be staying at home. Guilt that you are too strict with your children, or guilt that you are too soft. If you are having lots of negative feelings about parenting, you will then feel guilty about having such feelings. Guilt can crop up in just about anything you do. If you are not feeling guilty about your children, or yourself, then you may be feeling guilty about someone else.

> *'I feel guilty about my husband. I have no time to give him; it is easier not even to put him in the equation. If he gets home early and tries to help with the children's homework it makes things more complicated. I tell him to go away and then feel bad about it.'*

Some people become almost paralysed by their feelings of guilt, worry and self-doubt when it comes to parenting. Try to keep things in perspective and to think clearly and in a positive light. Remember, you will not be the first or last to be feeling as you do. Think of what will make you feel better and, although it is easier said than done, try to put it into action.

'A good night's sleep really helps me put things into perspective.'

Comparison to others

Some mothers can start to compare themselves to other mothers. From these comparisons can stem many different emotions. You may have heard comments similar to these:

- 'She has all that help and doesn't even work.'
- 'What is the point of having children if you are working all the time and never see them?'
- 'I couldn't stay at home with the children. I would get so bored. I don't know how you do it.'
- 'I wish I could stay at home, rather than having to go out to work.'

These comments may stem from self-justification, envy or from insecurity about the choices people have made about working and childcare. You make your own choices based on what you believe, what you and your family need – and more often than not on what your income and budget dictate. Again, everyone is different, some will enjoy going back to work, others will not.

'I am a much better parent when I work. If I am at home all the time with them I get wound up and feel claustrophobic and no one has a nice time. The best balance is working part time and then I can't wait to see my children when I come home and they are really excited too. I don't admit this to a lot of people as they tend to look a bit shocked.'

Also, we all learn as we go along. You may have thought you could work part time while your baby slept, and then realised that your plan had a few very loud and demanding flaws in it. You have to make the best decisions you can make at the time and do what you feel is right for you and your family, under the circumstances. Remember to listen to yourself, not others.

'When it goes wrong at work, you would rather be at home with the children and when you are with the children and it is chaos, you would rather be at work. The grass always seems greener on the other side!'

Other people's feelings

What about the highs and lows of everyone else in your home? How is your oldest child reacting to a new baby? Or to starting school? How is your partner reacting to you having given up work? To the fact you are having twins?

The emotions of everyone in your family need to be considered. As mentioned earlier, your responsibilities as a parent include the emotional well-being of your children. You need to work at meeting these, while at the same time keeping your relationship with your partner strong through the ups and downs of family life. And you wonder why so many TV ads depict mothers juggling or spinning plates?

Feelings about childcare

Just when you thought the parental rollercoaster could not get any more extreme, you take the plunge into childcare. Remember that it is utterly normal to feel positive and negative emotions about both parenting and childcare.

- **Positive not negative:** When it comes to our children we are expected to feel lots of positive and few negative emotions – we can therefore feel guilty when we experience some negative emotions.
- **Negative not positive:** When it comes to using childcare we are meant to feel lots of negative emotions about giving the care of our children to someone else and few positive emotions – we can therefore feel guilty when we experience positive emotions.

Positive emotions

Here are some of the positive feelings that you may have when someone else looks after your children:

- Freedom to work, to get things done or have time for yourself.
- Less financial worry as a result of being able to work.
- Increased fulfilment through resuming your career or starting a new one.
- Calm because you are less tense, stressed or pressured.
- Happiness as result of being a more positive parent.

  'I feel I have a better relationship with my children. I am not as fraught'.

- Relief at having a break from your children.

  'Childcare gives me sanity, more time and a chance to get my head above the chaos.'

Negative emotions

There are also, of course, negative emotions connected with asking someone else to look after your children. These may include:

- Sadness at missing out on their precious first years and all-important achievements.

  'I shouldn't be at work, I should be watching them grow up.'

- Worry, particularly over safety issues.
- Resentment that you need to go to work or use childcare.
- Concern that you are doing the wrong thing.

  'I have no past experiences of nannies in my life. Will my children have a massive complex when they are older?'

- Jealousy that your childcare provider gets to spend special time with your child and jealousy of the attachment your child forms with them.

  'I am not the sole recipient of their emotions and love.'

- Inadequacy that you should need childcare at all.

  'I should be a better mother, I should be able to do this by myself, but I can't.'

- Guilt about your childcare provider, particularly if you use in-home childcare or a childminder.

  'If I have had enough of them and they are my children, what must she be feeling?'

Emotions about your childcare may also encompass feelings about your partner. Many mothers (but by no means all, I hasten to add!) find that most of the responsibility for childcare falls upon them. They have to make the majority of childcare arrangements and do most handovers and pick-ups, while they feel their partners are free to come and go as they please.

As with your feelings about parenting you must not get too bogged down by your feelings about childcare. Take these three steps:

- Recognise what your feelings are.
- Think about why you have them.
- Accept them or take action to deal with them.

Responsibility to your childcarer

As you begin to use childcare, your responsibilities will again increase. Whatever type of childcare you decide to use you will have some sort of responsibility towards the person or people involved. While they are, of course, different from the responsibilities you have towards your child, the Hierarchy of Needs (see page 14) is still relevant. Fulfilling these needs will not only help your childcarer, but also you and your child.

Childcarers in your home

You can assess your responsibilities towards a nanny, au pair, relative or friend by considering their needs.

1 **Physiological (or basic) needs:** They need food, water and warmth.
2 **Need for safety:** They need a safe place to work.
3 **Need for love, affection and to belong:** Childcarers may not need your love, but they do need to feel that they belong and are welcome in your home and in your life.
4 **Need for esteem:** Childcarers carry out a very important job, and must be treated with respect. Always deal with them in a respectful manner and pay them the right amount at the right time.
5 **Need for self-actualisation:** If childcarers are given help to develop their skills, they will be able to reach their full potential. If they do things well, they will get more fulfilment in their job and develop their career, while you will have more freedom and peace of mind.

Out-of-home childcare

The same needs can be applied to the slightly different circumstances of a nursery, crèche, pre-school or childminder. However, you do not need to worry about their more basic needs.

1 **Physiological (or basic) needs:** This is their responsibility not yours.
2 **Need for safety:** This is their responsibility not yours.
3 **Need for love, affection and to belong:** It is important that they know the important part they play in your life. This will also rub off on your children.
4 **Need for esteem:** Show that you value and respect your childcarer and the service they are providing: • Do what they ask – label your child's belongings and so on. • Give them warning of changes of plan. • Drop off and pick up on time and always thank them. • Ensure you pay them the right amount at the right time.
5 **Need for self-actualisation:** Help them to be the best they can be. Let them know when you are pleased with what they are doing and also if you think something can be improved.

Thinking about emotions

The baby is still crying and your 'to do' list is longer than your arm, so what is the point of thinking about all these responsibilities and emotions? Firstly, it should help you to be aware of the amazing aspects of parenthood and to enjoy all those happy moments in your family. But also, if you can better understand what people need and why someone is reacting in a certain way, you will be better able either to accept or tackle any issues. You cannot solve a problem if you do not understand what you, or others, are feeling and why. It helps you to address the cause of a problem, not the symptom, for example, your toddler's tantrums brought on by the arrival of a new sibling. Greater awareness is a key step to happiness – it helps you to enjoy the good and address the not so good.

The more you work at being aware of others' emotions, particularly in your household, the easier it becomes – until it becomes second nature. It is very important that you look at your own emotions head on. Admit them to yourself, if not to anyone else – it is unhealthy not to. However, you may also find it helps to talk things through with your partner or a friend. If you can understand the reasons why you are feeling so worked up and frustrated, you can then do something about it.

> *'If I am having a laugh or a cuddle with the children, I try to stop and savour it. It is good to be aware of the good bits – I don't stop to think about them enough.'*

Bringing up children can be hard, the cost of living is high and sacrifices sometimes need to be made. We are not always living the perfect life and children are not always little angels. It is therefore understandable that when it comes to parenting and using childcare we will feel both positive and negative emotions. Deal with the negative and make sure you really enjoy the positive.

> *'I think people beat themselves up a lot, you just have to accept what you feel and get on with life.'*

You are important too!

All parents, and particularly mothers, need to remember that they are important too and need to get what they want from life – your life should not automatically be put on hold for the next 18 years. A home is happy when everyone in it is happy. Totally sacrificing your needs and wants for the sake of others is not a healthy way to live. Know the type of person you are and seek to get what you need from life, without, of course, totally abandoning your post of motherhood! Feeling happier and more fulfilled will help to make your home and family happier too.

Test your attitude to parenting and childcare

This simple questionnaire can help you to identify your attitude to parenting and childcare, which will then help you to make the right choices in childcare and work well with your choice. Three main styles of parenting have been identified and there are ideas and tips throughout the book on how to work with each type of childcare in line with your more dominant style or styles.

Circle **one** response for each question, either a, b or c. Although you may like to circle more than one, try to choose the answer that describes you best. There are no right or wrong answers.

1 **Which statement applies to your family the most?**
   a We are a very safety-conscious family.
   b We don't like things to be too structured.
   c Set rules and routines work really well for our family.

2 **Which statement best describes you?**
   a I like things done properly.
   b Life is too short to get worked up about the little things.
   c I will ask what is wrong if I feel someone is unhappy about something.

3 **When you are away from your children (not necessarily when they are with childcare), which statement applies to you most?**
   a I worry about whether they are okay.
   b I don't think about them too much but hope they are having fun.
   c I like to know that their routine is being followed.

4 **When leaving your children with childcare, which statement applies to you most?**
   a I am more relaxed if I know the person/nursery is well qualified/ accredited.
   b Once the children are settled and happy with childcare I am free to get on with my day.
   c I hope they are behaving but also learning something.

5 **What is your attitude to childcare?**
   a I sometimes worry about whether using it will have a long-term effect on my children.
   b It is a great thing and I am a better/calmer parent for it.
   c It teaches independence.

6 What are your thoughts on rules and boundaries?
  a Rules and boundaries should be there to keep children safe.
  b I can see their benefit but there should not be too many of them.
  c Set rules and boundaries make things easier for everyone.

7 What are your views on discipline for your children?
  a I think children need strong guidance rather than strict discipline.
  b I am happy to let the smaller things go.
  c The rules should be clear and children should know there are consequences.

8 What are your views on your childcarer disciplining your child?
  a I don't think they should be too strict as I think this can have an adverse effect.
  b I would leave it up to their discretion and unless it was serious I'd be happy not to know about it.
  c It is important. I like to know my rules are being followed even if I am not there.

9 How do you think children should be motivated?
  a Ensuring your children are happy will help to motivate them.
  b Through incentives, rewards and praise.
  c They need both praise and punishment.

10 How would you tackle an issue with your childcare?
  a I would act immediately without much thought, particularly if I was concerned about safety.
  b I would let the smaller things go.
  c I would discuss it and also offer ideas to stop it happening again.

What is your parenting style?

Count up the number of a, b and c answers that you gave. This will indicate your style of parenting. You may find that you have a mixture of styles, but your highest score or scores will show your stronger preference. There is no style that is better than another, however the ideal is to have a mixture – rather than be too extreme in any one style.

Keep them safe (mainly a)

You like things to be done properly. However, this can lead you to overload yourself, so be sure to ask for help when you need it.

When it comes to looking after your children you often feel that no one can do it better than you. Quite understandably, you can worry about their safety when you're not with them. At times this can stop you from concentrating on, or enjoying, what you are doing. Knowing your children are being looked after by a reputable and trusted childcarer will help to ease this worry.

You can also tend to worry about the effect that using childcare or using strict discipline can have on your children. Be careful not to over-indulge your children as a result. In extreme cases this can lead to a child taking the more dominant role away from the parent.

Freedom (mainly b)

You don't like things to be too structured and have a fairly relaxed and easy-going attitude. You can tend to shy away from confrontation, often feeling that life is too short.

You feel that childhood should be about being carefree and having fun. You feel that positive reward and praise will build up a child's confidence and independence. However, you do have your boundaries and limits about unacceptable behaviour. Always ensure you are consistent with these. Sometimes a fairly laid-back parent will suddenly become very strict if pushed too far – this kind of extreme swing can be confusing for a child or childcarer.

Once you have chosen the right childcare, you are happy for them to take over the reins and get on with it. Ensure that you are not too relaxed about things. While giving your children or your childcare freedom is a very positive thing, too much freedom can lead to your children resenting boundaries and your childcare becoming complacent.

Traditional (mainly c)

Increasingly (and maybe to your surprise), you are finding that you have quite a traditional outlook on life. You feel that you should continually strive to improve and learn from your experiences. You like your children to be seen to behave well. You want to instil in them the foundations of good manners and behaviour that will hold them in good stead for life.

You find that set routines and boundaries work well for your family. You believe in a combination of fair punishment and praise, and that children should understand the implications of their behaviour. Those who are too overbearing with their children may find they have frequent battles and/or power struggles. Remember that some of life's lessons can also be learnt through fun, games and family jokes.

When it comes to childcare, you want to know your children's routines are being followed and that they are not being allowed to get away with too much – something that could undo the efforts you put in yourself. If you have a very high number of 'c's, ensure that you praise both your children and your childcarer when it is due, and don't just focus on the things that need improving.

CHAPTER 2

Your Children

This chapter looks at the needs that your children will have over time, including:

- Their developmental milestones and the needs associated with these.
- Their safety needs at different ages.
- How your childcare needs may change over time.
- Considerations for children with special needs.
- An overview of the research on childcare and its effects on development.

The best for your child

We all want to do the best for our children and ensure they reach their maximum potential. Outlined on the following pages are some of the milestones that your children will reach over the years and the main needs they will have. As the main carers, you, your partner and your childcarer should ensure these are met. A good childcarer should always put the needs of the children in their care first and help them to reach their developmental milestones in a fun and caring way.

Before you get out your clipboard and start frantically ticking off what your child has and has not achieved, remember that these milestones should be used as a guide only. If you are concerned about your child's development, for any reason, talk to your GP or health visitor.

What they are doing	What they need
0–3 months	**0–3 months**
<ul><li>Sleep a lot to begin with.</li><li>Become very attached to main carer.</li><li>Turn head to sounds.</li><li>Will begin to smile.</li><li>Kick arms and legs.</li><li>Try to lift head.</li><li>Possibly roll from side onto back.</li><li>Make gurgling sounds as well as crying.</li><li>Explore things by putting them in their mouth.</li></ul>	<ul><li>Lots of eye contact and smiles.</li><li>Lots of cuddling to make them feel safe.</li><li>To hear lots of talk about things around them and what you are doing.</li><li>Stimulation with different textures, sounds and toys.</li><li>Suspended toys that they can reach up to.</li><li>A safe floor area to wriggle around on.</li><li>A simple daily routine that suits them and you.</li></ul>
3–9 months	**3–9 months**
<ul><li>Will usually have doubled from birth weight by 6 months.</li><li>Become attached to secondary carers.</li><li>Have clear likes and dislikes.</li><li>Will be weaned onto solids and begin to eat finger foods.</li><li>Can roll over and can sit unaided.</li><li>Will probably be crawling.</li><li>May be standing and possibly cruising between pieces of furniture.</li><li>Drop things and then look for them.</li><li>Transfer things in and out of containers.</li><li>Recognise names of family members.</li><li>Enjoy simple games.</li><li>Babble with sounds of one and two syllables.</li><li>May begin to show separation anxiety.</li><li>Have little or no sense of danger.</li></ul>	<ul><li>Lots of opportunities to play and explore – put toys just out of reach to encourage rolling and crawling.</li><li>A very safe environment, as they are now on the move!</li><li>A very close eye kept on them at all times.</li><li>A good balanced diet.</li><li>To hear lots of talk – pointing out people and objects.</li><li>To hear simple words repeated.</li><li>Encouragement to babble back to you.</li><li>Simple games and rhymes with actions</li><li>Books read with them.</li><li>Encouragement to explore new toys.</li><li>Familiarity with the childcarer they are left with – let them know when you are leaving and do so in a cheery manner with little fuss (this minimises separation anxiety).</li></ul>

What they are doing	What they need
9–18 months	**9–18 months**
• Will usually have tripled their birth weight by 12 months. • Become frustrated if they do not get their own way or are unable to do something. • May reach a peak in separation anxiety between 9 and 14 months. • Are very mobile – crawling, bottom-shuffling or walking. • Can go upstairs, but are not good at coming down. • Can build a simple two-brick tower. • Enjoy songs and rhymes with actions. • Hold a cup and are becoming more adept at feeding themselves. • Follow simple commands. • Start to say up to 20 simple words. • Use gestures to emphasise words. • Still have little or no sense of danger.	• A good balanced diet – keep presenting foods even if they do not appear to like them and keep introducing new foods. • Encouragement to feed themselves. • To be taught to go up and downstairs safely – down backwards on their hands and knees. • An eye kept on them at all times. • Help to understand dangers, 'Don't touch!', 'Ow!', 'Hot!'. • To hear simple words repeated and encouragement to copy you. • Books read with them – encourage them to point to objects and say the word or make the right sound. • Encouragement to use their imagination with simple role-play games. • All carers to use consistent rules and boundaries. • Separation anxiety dealt with in a no-fuss and cheery manner. • Help to understand the concepts of sharing and taking turns. • Opportunities to socialise with children of similar ages.

What they are doing	What they need
18–24 months	**18–24 months**
• Start to assert their independence, wanting to do things for themselves. • Can show strong preferences for things. • Are able to feed themselves fairly well. • Can scribble with a crayon. • Can build a simple three- or four-brick tower. • Can do simple jigsaws. • Enjoy ride-on toys. • Enjoy climbing activities. • Play alongside other children. • Point to things they want. • Begin to concentrate for longer stretches of time. • Have a steadily increasing vocabulary (200+ words). • Use short sentences, e.g. 'Doggy gone'.	• The chance to make decisions – give them choices. • A good balanced diet – keep presenting foods they may seem not to like and encourage them to try new things. • The opportunity to see how toys work – show them what to do, encourage them to do the same and then leave them to play and explore by themselves. • Encouragement to talk you through their favourite books. • Consistent rules and boundaries. • Encouragement to use their imagination and creativity through role play and dressing up. • Help with talking – repeat sentences back to them in the correct way but always with an encouraging tone, 'That's right, well done – the dog has gone'. • An eye kept on them at all times – some may have really caught the climbing bug!

What they are doing	What they need
2–3 years	2–3 years
• Become more adept at running. • Are usually potty trained by 2½–3 years. • Walk down stairs holding on to a rail. • Can kick a ball. • Can learn to pedal a tricycle. • Continue to enjoy climbing frames. • Can undress but may need help to dress. • Mostly play alongside other children. • Have an increasingly large vocabulary (300+ words) and more complex sentence construction. • Point to and name objects in books. • Ask a lot of questions! • Enjoy stories and songs. • Become more aware of right and wrong. • Begin to enjoy imaginative play.	• The opportunity to make decisions – give them choices. • Encouragement to learn through play – suggest games and things to do with toys. • Opportunities to play simple counting games – e.g. count when walking up and down the stairs. • Introduction to simple concepts such as smaller and bigger, on top of and underneath. • Encouragement to recognise shapes and colours. • Consistent discipline, rules and boundaries. • Encouragement to use creativity and fine motor skills – simple drawing and arts and crafts. • Opportunities to socialise with other children and form friendships. • Continued reinforcement of the concepts of sharing and taking turns. • Greater awareness of the world around them and their everyday life – 'What do we need to buy at the shops?' • Encouragement to begin to express their feelings.

Your children

What they are doing	What they need
3–4 years	**3–4 years**
• Can undress and usually dress themselves. • Are able to run well. • Are increasingly good at throwing and catching a ball. • Have improved climbing skills and balance. • Can hold a pencil well and draw simple pictures. • Can use scissors. • Play increasingly well with other children. • Can articulate their needs and ask for help. • Can talk about past events. • Can follow simple instructions. • Begin to take an interest in letters and numbers. • Enjoy imaginative play. • Speak increasingly clearly in sentences of four to six words or more. • Understand the concept of counting.	• Opportunities to play with other children and form and consolidate friendships. • Encouragement to begin to recognise letters and numbers – but ensure it is fun. • Opportunities to write their name – write their name in dots (indicating where to start each letter) and encourage them to write over the top. • Encouragement to link sounds to letters. • Encouragement to begin to work with numbers, e.g. 'How many plates do we need to get out for lunch?'. • Opportunities to make decisions through choices or to suggest what they would like to eat, do or wear. • Consistent rules and boundaries. • Opportunities to help you with simple daily tasks. • Encouragement to dress themselves. • Encouragement to think about concepts and ask relevant questions. • Fun, fun, fun with creativity and role play. • Increased awareness of the world around them, e.g. talk about the different seasons. • Encouragement to express their feelings and think about those around them.

What they are doing	What they need
4–5 years	**4–5 years**
<ul><li>By their fourth birthday, most children are double the height of their birth length.</li><li>Are very good at running and jumping, and getting better at hopping and skipping.</li><li>Have good pencil skills.</li><li>Have good verbal skills and sentence construction.</li><li>Can follow more detailed instructions.</li><li>Can talk about their feelings and ideas.</li><li>Enjoy rhyming and beginning to play with language.</li><li>Are interested in reading.</li><li>Continue to enjoy imaginative play.</li><li>Are increasingly aware of the needs and feelings of others.</li></ul>	<ul><li>Help to understand decisions – explain the reasons and feelings behind them.</li><li>Help to be made aware of people's feelings.</li><li>Encouragement with simple games involving numbers and letters – but do not push too much.</li><li>Lots of books read to them and the chance to start reading to you.</li><li>Games, climbing frames and obstacle courses to help increase their balance and physical dexterity.</li><li>Opportunities to join activity classes, e.g. ballet, football, tag rugby.</li><li>Some leeway when they start school as they will find it very exhausting to begin with.</li><li>Encouragement to express their feelings and express their thoughts on the feelings of those around them.</li></ul>
5–8 years	**5–8 years**
<ul><li>Start to lose baby teeth.</li><li>Can undress and dress themselves.</li><li>Can hit a ball with a bat.</li><li>Can ride a bicycle.</li><li>Learn to read and write.</li><li>Enjoy working with numbers.</li><li>Enjoy simple jokes.</li><li>Enjoy games with rules.</li><li>Can concentrate for much longer periods.</li><li>Are keen to learn and assimilate information.</li></ul>	<ul><li>An interest to be shown in their learning at school – always help with and encourage their homework.</li><li>Opportunities to increase their learning through play, e.g. playing post offices and writing letters and counting out money for stamps.</li><li>Congratulations for their successes, but not too much made of their failures – they can be sensitive.</li></ul>

Your child as an individual

You also need to think about your child's individual needs. For example, is he or she very shy, very physically active or lacking in confidence when it comes to trying new things? To help children flourish, their individual needs have to be taken into consideration. Think about what your child needs. Is it encouragement and confidence building; a chance to get rid of excess energy; fairly strong rules and boundaries to curb unruly behaviour? It is up to you to help your children be the best they can be, and this includes finding the right childcare to suit them.

Any good childcarer should see your child as an individual, but it is also your responsibility to make your childcarer aware of your child's needs, or any worries that you have. This will help them to do their best for your child. Hopefully, you will see your child flourish accordingly. It is extremely rewarding for a childcarer to see a child turn a corner and know that they helped to make it happen.

Keeping them safe

We have already established that safety is a basic need for children. You may feel that your home is a fairly safe environment already, but you need to look at it from the point of view of a baby or toddler. There may be dangers you have not noticed and these dangers combined with increasingly mobile and curious little people have the potential to lead to disaster.

Often when you think you have made everything super safe, your child will move on to the next stage and find a whole other world of excitement … and danger.

Now for the really sobering stuff! According to the Royal Society for the Prevention of Accidents (RoSPA):

- Accidental injuries are the most common cause of death in children over one year of age. Every year these injuries leave many thousands of children permanently disabled or disfigured.
- Over 1 million children under the age of 15 experience serious accidents in and around the home every year.
- Those most at risk from a home accident are in the 0–4 years age group. Falls account for the majority of non-fatal accidents while the highest number of deaths is due to fire.
- The largest number of accidents happens in the living/dining room. However, the most serious accidents happen in the kitchen and on the stairs. Every year over 67,000 children experience an accident in the kitchen; of these children, 43,000 are aged between 0 and 4 years. Each year 58,000 children have accidents on the stairs.

There is, however, some good news from RoSPA too:

- Most of these accidents are preventable through increased awareness, improvements in the home and greater product safety.

Accidents in the home are frequent. Although many may happen when you have your back turned, or are in another room, others will happen right in front of your eyes when you just cannot move fast enough to prevent them.

Some people feel that they do not need to think about childproofing a house until their child starts to crawl at around 6 months old. At some point they are likely to be alerted by a scream and a thud to the fact their child has learnt to climb the stairs. Usually babies only fall from the first or second step, but it can be much worse. So get your large health-and-safety hat on sooner rather than later, and consider baby-proofing and toddler-proofing at the same time.

Childcare and safety

If you decide on in-home childcare, you need to ensure your home is as safe as possible. Don't leave it up to your nanny, au pair or mother-in-law to do it. You must do the safety checks on your home and then work as a team with your childcarer to ensure things are kept safe and new dangers are identified and dealt with.

If you decide on out-of-home childcare, you have the peace of mind that they have to adhere to strict safety guidelines and are well regulated by the Government. However, you also need to make sure you are happy with the measures they have in place.

While the need to keep your home safe for your children cannot be stressed enough, you must also avoid wrapping them up in too much cotton wool. They need to be able to learn to make their own safety decisions as they grow up.

Baby safety

You may think that a baby is less prone to accidents than a young and mobile child, but bear in mind the following:

- A newborn baby can wriggle and become wedged between, or under, sofa cushions.
- As soon as a baby can lift its head, it can bang it on the floor when, exhausted from the effort, it lies back down.

- As soon as a baby can roll over, it is able to move about a room. It can roll over to a socket, a fire, a small object or get jammed under a sofa or low table.

Here are some things you may like to consider, right from the start:

- Ensure the layout of your baby's room is sensible and safety oriented – no ties or straps near a cot, a changing mat that is near, or on, the floor to prevent a fall when nappy changing, no low tables below a window.
- Put covers on all sockets.
- Ensure your high chair and buggy have good straps.
- Ensure your child's first toys are all age relevant, and for further peace of mind double check that you think they are safe enough.
- Ensure that first clothes have no ties or straps.
- Do not allow your baby to get too hot or too cold.
- Ensure you have the correct car seat for your child's weight and that the seat is correctly installed.
- Ensure your house is not too hot, cold or damp.
- If you have cats or dogs, be prepared for them to be too loving to a new arrival or jealous.

Toddler-proofing

As your child begins to be more mobile, get down on your hands and knees and see the world from a toddler's perspective. To what would someone this size make a beeline to investigate? Invite a friend round with a very busy baby or marauding toddler and see what he or she finds of particular interest. Between the ages of 1 and 2 you can pretty much guarantee that your child will be into everything. Toddler-proofing your home will most importantly keep your child safe and give you peace of mind, but it will also keep your home safe.

> *'She had poured a whole bottle of dark nail varnish over the new cream carpet.'*

The stakes are raised and your toddler is on a mission. You need to be constantly vigilant and should pay particular attention to the following:

- Ensure windows, particularly those upstairs, are fully childproofed.
- Keep flexes out of reach, especially those on kettles and irons.
- Put locks on cupboards and drawers, particularly those containing knives, glasswear or cleaning products.
- Keep all medicines out of reach. You may feel a vitamin pill is not a danger, but a child could choke on it or it may affect their metabolism. If your child eats one and enjoys it, he or she may move onto other drugs if they are within reach.

- Keep razors, knives and scissors out of reach and out of sight.
- Ensure that front doors and garden gates are secure.
- Keep children away from ponds or if you have one in the garden ensure that it is made safe. Ensure buckets and sandpits don't fill up with rainwater. Never leave a toddler alone with a paddling pool of water.
- Be aware of the potential danger of dog leads, strings or straps on coats and cords on window blinds.
- Keep all small objects out of reach, including small parts of toys belonging to older children.
- Keep all make-up, shampoos and any other gooey stuff out of reach.

'I love it when we get back home from visiting other people. You can let the children run around and you know they are safe and they can't damage anything. Visiting can be exhausting. You are constantly on your guard, worried about your children and your friends' possessions.'

Getting older

Children over the age of 4 are slightly less curious and also have a greater understanding of the consequences of their actions. They can understand, for example, that the products in the cleaning cupboard could make them very sick. They like games with rules and they also like life with rules. Things make sense and they can feel important and included by sticking to these rules. However, they are still young and exploring the world, so you should always be on your guard. They enjoy independent and imaginative play and do not want you watching them the entire time, but you should always know what they are up to.

- They may decide to pack a rucksack, climb over the garden fence and go on an adventure.
- They may decide to help themselves to fruit or make a sandwich and to cut it up with a sharp knife.
- They may decide it would be nice to try and make mummy a cup of tea.

Yikes! The possible consequences of these are terrifying. You need to ensure you keep things as secure as possible and that your children know the safety rules and what will happen if they are broken. Make sure you keep checking on what they are doing as the old rule will always apply: if things are quiet, be worried, be very worried … they are up to something.

And don't be fooled into thinking there will come a time when you can stop worrying. Before you know it, you will be lying awake in the small hours waiting to hear their car return home after a night out. Once again, welcome to parenthood!

Changing needs

Making your first childcare decisions can be hard and quite daunting. However, decisions will become easier over the years, as your experience and confidence grow. Your childcare needs will change over time, increasing as more children come along and decreasing as your children go to school and grow older. But even when your children are of school age, some holiday and after-school cover may still be needed.

It is highly likely that you will use a number of different forms of childcare over the years. Keep your mind open to the different options – you may be surprised by what you use and how your perceptions change. Only with an open mind can you make the best childcare decisions for your children and their needs.

> *'I had never agreed with nannies, but when the twins came along it was too much to get everyone out and to nursery in the mornings and also bedtime seemed to be getting later and later and noisier and noisier, so we took the plunge. We only had a nanny for a year but it was the best decision at the time, making life a lot more bearable for everyone!'*

This is an example of one family's decisions about childcare over time.

The children	The mother	The childcare
Jack: baby	Six months' maternity leave, then back to work full time.	**Jack:** childminder five days a week following maternity leave.
Emma: baby **Jack:** toddler	Six months' maternity leave then back to work three days a week.	**Jack:** to childminder three days a week. **Emma:** at home for maternity leave then childminder three days a week.
Tom: baby **Emma:** toddler **Jack:** pre-school	Give up work for 18 months.	**Tom:** baby at home. **Emma:** childminder two mornings a week. **Jack:** pre-school three mornings a week.

The children	The mother	The childcare
Tom: toddler **Emma:** pre-school **Jack:** school	Back to work three days a week.	**Tom:** nursery three days a week. **Emma:** nursery three days a week; nursery also drops her at and collects her from pre-school three mornings a week. **Jack:** school five days a week and nursery and holiday clubs during holidays.
Tom: pre-school **Emma:** school **Jack:** school	Back to work four days a week.	**Tom:** pre-school four mornings a week and au pair in afternoons. **Jack and Emma:** at school and au pair after school; au pair and holiday clubs in holidays.
Tom: school **Emma:** school **Jack:** school	Back to work full time	All children at school; use grandparents, after-school and holiday clubs as wrap-around care.

Special needs

The term special needs covers a vast spectrum, from learning difficulties and behavioural problems to severe mental and physical disabilities. Some children will be diagnosed very early on and start to receive immediate help. For others it may be the parent or indeed a childcarer who senses that a child is not reaching the appropriate milestones at the appropriate times. If you are concerned about your child, for any reason, it is important that you follow this up. The sooner a child can be given help the better. Early intervention can make a tremendous difference, and may even eradicate the problem entirely.

From 2008 to 2011, the Government will be investing £340m in services for children with special needs, with £35m of this going towards increasing accessible childcare. However, you will still need to work out what you think is the best childcare solution for you and your family. You may not have been planning to use childcare, but often parents find that with a special needs child they need more help not only for that child, but also for other children, or indeed to give themselves a break.

'You need more help than you realise, you need to meet people, and research nurseries and schools thoroughly, and can't do it properly when you have your children around you. There is also so much admin associated with a special needs child. I must make about 30 phone calls a week about things like finding the right equipment, chasing physios and just asking questions.'

Childcare decisions are hard, and they can be particularly hard if you have a child with special needs. However, like all decisions, if you have the right information you can usually make a good and well-informed choice.

It is very important that before looking for childcare you are extremely clear on your child's diagnosis, and what this means in terms of daily needs and yearly goals. You can then work out which are the best options for your child and discuss particular needs with your potential childcarer.

'Get involved in a parent support group. They are the best source of information, particularly the local ones.'

Your local council will have a Children's Disability Team who will assess your child and decide on the care and help that your child needs. Depending on your child's diagnosis, you may be given help with in-home childcare. You may be given a carer who will help to look after your child or, alternatively, direct payments for you to spend on childcare that you source yourself. If your child's disability is severe you may be given 24-hour care.

'We received money, rather than a carer, which I preferred as I felt I could make it go further. We employed an au pair who could help with my other children as well, so I could also spend one-on-one time with my daughter.'

As your child gets older you will probably start thinking about nursery schools, day nurseries, pre-schools or playgroups. Attending a good nursery or pre-school could be really beneficial to your child and may even decrease the amount of extra help needed later on. Depending on the extent of your child's needs, he or she may be assessed and given a Statement of Special Educational Needs (SEN).

Early education settings such as day nurseries, nursery schools and pre-schools have to abide by the Special Educational Needs Code of Practice. It helps them to identify, assess and provide help for children with special needs and sets out the processes and procedures that they should follow. Contact the Department for Children, Schools and Families (see Useful

Sources of Information) for a copy of the SEN Code of Practice.

Early education settings place great importance on identifying special educational needs early so that they can help children as much as possible. You can appeal against the SEN statement if you don't agree with it either in terms of what it offers as help or in how it has assessed your child's needs. Each school or nursery should have a Special Educational Needs Co-ordinator (SENCO). Do not be afraid to speak up about what your child needs in order that the help provided is of maximum benefit to your child. Ensure that the setting has enough staff to give your child the time and attention required.

> *'You often have to fight to get what you feel is right for your child. You have to be persuasive, you have to get on with people and work the system to your child's benefit.'*

The options for nursery or pre-school for special needs children are usually one of the following:

- Mainstream early education setting with added support from the staff.
- Mainstream early education setting with a dedicated assistant.
- Mainstream early education setting that has a special needs unit and staff.
- A dedicated special needs early education setting.

> *'It is even more important with childcare for a special needs child that you meet everyone who will help to care for your child.'*

Some nurseries, pre-schools and childminders may not have cared for a child with special needs previously but may be willing to take them on. While a welcoming and inclusive attitude is very important, true capability, expectations and experience are equally important. Make sure they really can do the best for your child.

In this book, each chapter that deals with a specific type of childcare gives details of its suitability for children with special needs.

Truth or scare?

It seems that every few weeks there is a new study outlining the terrible effects of childcare on your children. Guilt raises its ugly head again and you question what you are doing with your life and the lives of your precious children.

There is no doubt that research is extremely useful and will hopefully help to improve all types of childcare. However, as childcare is such an emotive issue, any negative aspects found in research are immediate headline grabbers, while the positive effects are less likely to make the front pages. Ultimately, it is up to you to try to make the best decision for your child based on your circumstances, the information available and your own instincts.

Some research to date

Let's start with some of the positive stuff. The Effective Provision of Pre-School Education (EPPE) project in the UK looked at a combination of settings including local authority day nurseries, playgroups, private day nurseries, nursery schools and nursery classes. They found that attending these settings improved all children's development compared with those who had no pre-school attendance; the group with no attendance had poorer cognitive skills, sociability and concentration when they started primary school. They also found that an early start between the ages of 2 and 3 was linked with better intellectual skills and sociability.

However, they did conclude that the quality of the setting has an impact on these results. Children were seen to make more progress in settings with staff that have higher qualifications, where there were warm interactive relationships with the children and where educational and social development were seen to be of equal importance. The highest achievements were found in those settings that integrated both care and education, and in nursery schools.

'It makes beginning primary school really easy.'

The Institute of Education found that achievement in language, reading and numeracy increases in proportion to time spent in pre-school. This means that by the age of 5, children can be four to six months ahead of their peers who did not attend. The benefits of a good pre-school grounding have been proven to be beneficial well into primary school and beyond.

However, on the negative side, in April 2007 Oxford University and the Institute for Fiscal Studies found that children under 3 years of age who spend more than 35 hours a week in nursery showed higher levels of antisocial behaviour and anxiety.

The National Institute of Child Health and Human Development (NICHD) in the USA reported in 2007 that children are more likely to be antisocial and aggressive if they spend most of their day in a nursery. However, they have also reported that good early years childcare has been linked to better academic scores including increases in vocabulary. But this positive effect was reported to wear off for children spending over 30 hours in nursery a week.

The NICHD study authors suggest that correlations between nursery care and behaviour problems could be due to a lack of training, and time to deal with problems and conflict that arise in a nursery situation. It would follow that ensuring a childcare provider has sufficient and well-trained staff will help to lessen the possible negative effects of nursery-based care.

Research at the University of California also suggests that children who attend day care or playgroups cut their risk of contracting the most common type of childhood leukaemia by 30 per cent. They believe this is because the childhood infections they encounter in these environments challenge the immune system, thereby decreasing the chance of inappropriate response to subsequent infections.

What's the conclusion?

There is evidence of both positive and negative effects of childcare for pre-school children. It has been shown that good-quality provision can enhance all-round development, while bad-quality provision, teamed with long hours away from home, could have a negative effect. The main findings are:

- Pre-school experience, compared to none, enhances all-round development.
- An earlier start (under age 3 years) is related to better intellectual development.
- Full-time attendance leads to no better gains for children than part-time.
- Some settings are more effective than others in delivering positive outcomes.
- Good quality can be found across all types of early years settings; however, quality was higher overall in settings integrating care and education and in nursery schools.
- Well-qualified staff have an impact as do warm and interactive relationships.

What you do is even more important

The majority of studies also point to the enormous benefit of parents encouraging their children in learning and activities at home to complement the efforts of their childcare. The NICHD study concluded that parenting quality is more important to development than the particular type, quantity or quality of childcare.

The Effective Provision of Pre-School Education (EPPE) project in the UK highlighted a range of activities at home that are all associated with even higher intellectual and social/behavioural scores, if coupled with pre-school attendance:

- Reading with your child.
- Teaching songs and rhymes.
- Painting and drawing.
- Playing with and teaching letters and numbers.
- Visiting the library.
- Taking your child on visits.
- Creating regular opportunities to play with friends at home.

CHAPTER 3

Childcare

Many people feel totally overwhelmed by the thought of finding suitable childcare. In home, out of home, nanny, au pair, nursery, housekeeper, childminder, granny… the choices seem endless. You would not be the first to say, having put your head above the parapet, that it all looks far too scary and complicated, thank you very much, and I might just stay at home with the little dears instead.

This chapter will help you overcome any apprehension and start working your way through the childcare maze. It will:

- Outline the pros and cons of both in-home and out-of-home childcare.
- Give a clear description of the main types of childcare, along with their pros and cons.
- Give you some thoughts on different combinations of childcare.
- Give a brief summary of Government activity and support in the area of childcare.

In-home versus out-of-home childcare

This may not be a decision that is relevant to you. You may have very strong feelings on the subject, have heard horror stories of live-in nannies or feel that the size of your house or budget is making the decision for you. Alternatively, it may be the first major decision for you to make, and once it is made you may feel the subsequent decisions fall into place with more ease. Pros and cons for both options are outlined on the following pages. To help your decision-making, mark a tick or a cross in the columns provided next to any points that really appeal to you or concern you.

Out-of-home childcare includes:

- Day nurseries, work nurseries/crèches.
- Nursery schools and pre-schools.
- Childminders.
- Out-of-school care.

Out-of-home pros	✓	Out-of-home cons	✗
Peace of mind that the child-care setting is Government regulated and regularly inspected.		If your children are ill you will have to stay at home or find alternative cover.	
Children start their education in line with the early years curriculum.		You are likely to be charged if your children are ill or away on holiday.	
Almost 100 per cent reliability – they are guaranteed to be open on the days they say they will and many open all year round.		Children may pick up more colds and bugs, meaning you have to take more time off work.	
Children are with other children of the same age and can form some very strong friendships.		You are constrained by drop-off and pick-up times, often with little flexibility.	
This can be the most affordable type of childcare.		Leaving a baby in a nursery setting or with a childminder can be stressful and worrying at first.	
You can often get financial assistance from the Government or your employer.		There are negative stories in the press about the effects of childcare, particularly nurseries, on children.	
Children are eligible for five free early years funding sessions per week from the age of 3.		It can take time for children to settle in – this can be a stressful time for both children and parents.	
They are equipped with lots of new toys and activities, which children love.		You have less control over your children's routine, diet and discipline.	
Children will be better prepared for school in terms of socialising, learning and a more formal routine.		Staff turnover can be high, which may be unsettling for children.	
Your home is your own!		Staff can be young and inexperienced.	

In-home childcare includes:

- Relatives and friends.
- Nannies, maternity and night nannies.
- Au pairs and mother's helps.

In-home pros	✓	In-home cons	✗
Help comes to you or lives in, ensuring greater flexibility in handover time and hours of cover.		If your childcare can't make it to work, you are left in the lurch and will have to make alternative arrangements, often at short notice.	
You are not constrained by nursery or childminder working hours.		You have someone in your home all day (or 24 hours a day) so lose your privacy.	
Children remain in their own environment and in their own routine.		It can take more time and effort to find someone you are happy to share your home with.	
If agreed upfront, they can help with other duties, e.g. shopping, housework.		You have to manage in-home childcare and ensure they are happy and fulfilled in their job.	
Your childcarer may provide over-night cover.		It is your responsibility as an employer to ensure all taxes and National Insurance are paid.	
Children can attend classes and activities selected by you, whether you are there to take them or not.		Your children may have less opportunity to socialise with other children.	
If you work from home you can see your children during the day.		You don't know what is going on when you are not there.	
Your children will have one-to-one attention with the same carer over time.		If you decide to provide a car with the job there will be the expense of the car, insurance and fuel.	
You have greater control over discipline, values and the food your children are given.		If the carer lives in you will forfeit a bedroom/flat and subject your home to additional wear and tear.	
Your children are less likely to pick up as many illnesses.		If you have only one child it can be an expensive form of childcare.	
You can build up a strong and fulfilling working relationship with the carer.		If things go wrong with the working relationship it can be very stressful for all concerned.	

Out-of-home childcare

Day and work nurseries

These are open all year round for up to 12 hours a day and will care for children from 6 weeks to 5 years old. They have to be Government registered and are inspected every one to three years. There are strict guidelines in relation to the staff-to-child ratio. The majority of nurseries will have between 20 and 50 children (although some can have up to 100). Children are usually separated into two or three groups such as babies, toddlers and pre-school and will have areas, toys and activities designed for each age group.

There are various different types of day nurseries:

- **Private:** These are run as a business or a charity. They may be part of a chain or a single independent nursery.
- **Community/neighbourhood:** These are run on a not-for-profit basis, and consequently their fees can be lower than those of private nurseries.
- **Work or college:** These are attached or linked to a specific company, university or college and provide care for the children of employees and/or students. They may also offer additional places if they have not filled them via their own employees or students.
- **Local authority:** Places are often subsidised or may even be free; you usually have to be referred by a GP, social worker or health visitor.
- **Children's Centre (Early Excellence Centre):** The Government's aim is to have a Children's Centre in every community by 2010. Built on the concept of Early Excellence Centres, they offer childcare for children under 5 years old, and have a qualified teacher who plans and oversees the children's activities. These centres also provide additional healthcare and family support, including job-seeking advice. It is likely that local authority nurseries, neighbourhood nurseries and Early Excellence Centres will all be combined into Children's Centres.
- **Crèche:** These provide occasional childcare, thus enabling a parent to undertake a particular activity, for example, sport, a doctor's appointment, shopping or just a quiet cup of coffee with a friend. Many leisure and shopping centres now have their own crèche. They have to be Government registered if they run for more than two hours a day, and those that are registered work to the same standards as nurseries and operate on the same adult-to-child ratio. Crèches are designed and therefore should be used for occasional rather than full-time care.
- **Montessori:** See page 51.

Suitable for:

- Children up to the age of 5 who will enjoy socialising with others. (Some nurseries do cater for children up to 8 years old after school or in the school holidays, see page 55).
- Small babies; the age at which nurseries take babies varies, the earliest being six weeks.
- Children of parents who work long hours or have a long commute, as they cover a wide span of hours. However, they often have little flexibility for late pick-up.
- Children of parents who need guaranteed reliability in their childcare.

A nursery may have a minimum attendance of two sessions per week, so may not be suitable for someone looking for one morning or afternoon of childcare a week; however, a local crèche could be ideal for this.

Day and work nursery pros	✓	Day and work nursery cons	✗
They have to be Government registered and are regularly inspected.		Places can be hard to find in well-regarded nurseries.	
Your children will be in a social environment and will learn how to interact and play well with other children.		You will have to keep your children at home if they are ill.	
They will usually follow the Government early years framework and curriculum. The day is structured with appropriate activities.		They may not be able to stick exactly to your children's routines.	
They are well equipped in terms of toys and crafts, with separate rooms or areas for different ages.		They can have a high staff turnover, which can be unsettling for children.	
They usually have high safety and hygiene standards.		There are negative stories in the press, about the effect of nurseries on young children.	
They have long opening hours during the day, which helps parents who are working long hours.		Few will tolerate late pick-ups, due to strict adult-to-child ratios: you are likely to be charged a late fee.	

Day and work nursery pros	✓	Day and work nursery cons	✗
All staff are Criminal Records Bureau checked. Some nurseries ensure their staff go through their own training scheme before starting.		Some may have quite young and inexperienced staff.	
You may be able to get some financial assistance from the Government or your employer and once children reach 3 they get five free early years funding sessions per week.		Fees can be high if using a private nursery, particularly if you have more than one child attending.	
They may do a drop-off and pick-up from pre-schools and schools.		Those in cities and town centres may have limited parking, which can make dropping off and picking up more stressful.	
They are usually open all year round.		Your preferred nursery may be some distance from your home.	

Nursery schools and pre-schools

These take children from approximately 2½ years old until school age and provide early education and childcare. They follow the same term and holiday patterns as schools and offer full-day or half-day sessions. They may be independent or linked to a state or private school. They have to be Government registered and are inspected every one to three years. If registered, they follow the appropriate early years curriculum. They teach basic numeracy, reading and writing in preparation for school. The staff will be a combination of trained teachers, classroom assistants and nursery nurses. Nursery schools generally take between 20 to 50 children and pre-schools between 10 and 20. If the setting is Government registered, you are able to claim the early years funding of five free sessions per week once your child is over 3 years of age.

There are several different types of nursery schools and pre-schools:

- **State or community nursery schools:** These are free, or offer subsidised places. They are funded by the local education authority and may be attached to a primary school. They will follow the appropriate early years curriculum. Children are taught in a fun atmosphere by a qualified teacher.
- **Private nursery schools:** These charge fees and are independently run. Most of them follow the early years curriculum. They may teach other subjects such as French and ballet.

- **Montessori nursery schools:** These are a form of private nursery school that uses the Montessori method, developed by Maria Montessori in the early 1900s. The Montessori method is based on child-directed learning. Children are allowed to choose what they wish to work with and to develop at their own pace – an approach that is known to work particularly well for both special needs and gifted children. This freedom of choice encourages independence as well as self-discipline. Children are encouraged to correct their own mistakes and great importance is placed on social interaction and respect for each other and their environment. They are also taught important practical skills such as dressing and undressing, laying the table and keeping their play areas clean. These may follow school opening hours and holidays or may work more like a day nursery and offer childcare up to 12 hours a day throughout the year. Many follow the early years curriculum.
- **Community pre-schools (also referred to as pre-school playgroups):** These charge fees but as they are usually run on a not-for-profit basis the fees are kept to a minimum. Parents are often involved in their running through a parents' committee. While they teach basic numeracy, reading and writing, many place great emphasis on learning through play. They may have their own building or use a village hall or community centre. Some have an hour-long break between morning and afternoon sessions, or may only be open in the mornings, making them unsuitable for all-day childcare.

Suitable for:

- Primarily children from 3 to 5 years old who are keen to socialise and learn.
- Some 2-year-olds. Places may be available for 2-year-olds, though they may need to have reached certain milestones, for example, potty trained and able to speak. Some take children below 2 years.

Some nurseries have a minimum attendance of two sessions a week, so may not be suitable for someone looking for one morning or afternoon of childcare a week.

Parents who are working full time and want their child to benefit from the social and educational aspects of a nursery school or pre-school will need to arrange additional wrap-around and holiday care, as their hours are usually limited to 9am to 3pm.

> *'They are just suddenly ready to learn about letters and numbers and you realise you don't have the time to do it yourself.'*

Nursery school and pre-school pros	✓	Nursery school and pre-school cons	✗
They have to be Government registered and are regularly inspected.		Most will not take children under 2½ years old.	
Your children are among others of their own age and learn how to interact and play well. They are likely to form some strong friendships.		Places can be hard to find in well-regarded nursery schools and pre-schools. You may need to live within the catchment area to get a place.	
Your children follow the appropriate early years curriculum, become accustomed to how a school works and get their education off to a good start.		You have to keep your children at home if they are ill.	
They are well equipped in terms of toys and equipment and the learning is suitably structured for the age of the children.		Younger children may find it hard to adjust to the routine and discipline of a school setting; you may feel they are being forced to grow up too soon.	
They usually have high safety and hygiene standards.		There are fewer adults to children than in other forms of childcare.	
The staff are usually well trained and experienced – are likely to be qualified teachers.		If working full time, you will need to find wrap-around care and holiday cover, as the majority do not offer full-time care.	
Research has pointed to the benefits of pre-school education.		There is no flexibility – the children have to be picked up when the session or day ends.	
You can help to run pre-school sessions which will involve you in your children's education and also the local community.		You may have to take time off work to fulfil your contribution to a pre-school.	
You may be able to get some financial assistance from the Government or your employer and once your children are old enough they are eligible for five free early years funding sessions a week.		Fees can be high if using a private nursery, particularly if you have more than one child attending.	

Nursery school and pre-school pros	✓	Nursery school and pre-school cons	✗
In a pre-school you can attend the first few sessions with your child if you want to.		Nurseries and pre-schools in cities and town centres may have limited parking, which can make dropping off and picking up more stressful.	
The nursery may feed into your preferred school and so your children become familiar with it before they start.		Your preferred nursery may be some distance from your home.	

Registered childminders

A registered childminder is someone who looks after up to six children under the age of 8, in England and Wales, and under the age of 12 in Scotland and Northern Ireland. They usually do this in their own home. They are registered under the 1989 Children's Act to ensure they meet a set standard. Inspection and registration are carried out by Ofsted in England, the Care and Social Services Inspectorate (CSSIW) in Wales, the Scottish Commission for the Regulation of Care in Scotland and the Health and Social Services Trust in Northern Ireland. Once they are registered, they are usually inspected every one to three years.

They must meet all the necessary regulations and training requirements for their area, including Criminal Records Bureau check, health check, appropriate insurance and first aid training. Their home is thoroughly checked to ensure it is safe and suitable for young children.

Childminders in a lot of areas can now deliver the early years curriculum which allows you to claim five free early years funding sessions per week.

Increasingly, individual childminders are joining up to networks. This allows them to share knowledge and experience and provide back-up to each other if they are ill or on holiday.

Suitable for:

- Children under school age.
- Children of school age if the childminder is happy to do drop-offs and pick-ups.
- Children with special needs if the childminder has the correct training and/or experience.
- Children whose parents work long or unusual working hours, if the childminder can accommodate these.

Registered childminder pros	✓	Registered childminder cons	✗
They have to be Government registered and are regularly inspected.		Recommended childminders are often fully booked up.	
Your children can socialise with other children and stay with their sibling(s).		The hours they have available may not match the ones you need.	
The adult-to-child ratio ensures your children will get enough one-on-one attention.		You may have to provide your children's meals or you may not be happy with what they are feeding your children.	
It is one of the cheaper forms of childcare and you may be able to get some financial assistance from the Government or your employer.		You will have to keep your children at home if they are ill (although childminders do sometimes offer a bit more flexibility than a nursery).	
Your children are looked after in a home setting – this can be reassuring if they are young.		In trying to accommodate the routines of all their charges they may not be able to exactly stick to your children's routines.	
They may do school or activity-group pick-up and drop-off and after-school care.		They may not have a guaranteed back-up if they are ill.	
Some childminding arrangements can last for years, giving children a good sense of security.		If under school age, your children may spend quite a lot of time in a buggy or car while the childminder runs errands or does pick-ups and drop-offs at school for other children.	
They are self-employed so you do not need to worry about paying their tax or National Insurance.		They may not be able to accommodate a growing family (e.g. if you have another baby and go back to work).	
They may be able to offer a degree of flexibility to suit your working hours and help out in a crisis.		There may be other members of the childminder's family around during the day. (Anyone over 16 in their home must be Criminal Records Bureau checked.)	

Registered childminder pros	✓	Registered childminder cons	✗
The majority will be parents (or grandparents) themselves.		If they are looking after their own child at the same time they may give preferential treatment.	
They will work all year round.		They are unlikely to take their holiday at the same time as you.	

Out-of-school care

Out-of-school care, also known as wrap-around care, provides quality childcare, primarily for children between 3 and 8 years old before and after school and during the school holidays. The Government's 'extended schools' initiative aims to see all schools offering wrap-around care on either side of the school day, between 8am and 6pm by 2010. The schools can do this themselves or in partnership with other voluntary or independent providers. Consequently it is a growing area, offering an increasing number of options.

If a form of out-of-school care is run for more than two hours a day for more than five days a year, it has to be Government registered. Some providers of out-of-school care also provide overnight care.

There are various forms:

- **Breakfast clubs and after-school clubs:** These are usually on school premises or close to them. They provide the opportunity for children to play, socialise, relax and do their homework rather than a formal education. If a breakfast club runs for less than two hours, it does not need to be registered.
- **Specific activity after-school clubs:** These extra-curricular activities (for example, ballet, drama, French) can last from 45 minutes to 1½ hours after the usual school closing time.
- **Holiday clubs:** These may be based at a school or a community or leisure centre. They include a whole host of activities and sports, for example, ceramics, arts and crafts, cookery, drama, photography and football. Children can do whole or half days. Some clubs also run theme weeks. Alternatively, they may be entirely dedicated to a particular skill or hobby, for example, football or drama.
- **Weekend clubs:** These are run on the same lines as a holiday club.
- **Open access schemes:** These are for older children. However, some will take children from as young as 5 years old. They are much less structured and tend to be in play centres and adventure playgrounds. They offer 'open access play' where no prior booking is required.

- **Other childcare:** Other forms of childcare, for example, childminders, day nurseries, friends or relatives, nannies or au pairs are often able to provide out-of-school care too.

Suitable for:

- Children of school age, although some will take children as young as 3.
- Children of parents who are both working full time or are studying.
- Children of parents who have to work weekend shifts (weekend clubs).

Out-of-school pros	✓	Out-of-school cons	✗
They have to be Government registered and are regularly inspected.		Most will not take children under 3 years old.	
They are usually in or close to the school. If in the school, it will be a familiar environment for your children.		It can result in a long day away from home. Children, particularly younger children, can be very tired by the end of the week.	
Your children are among their peers and are likely to strengthen some friendships.		They may only admit children that attend the school they are linked to.	
They have activities and equipment suitable for the age group and are usually good value for money.		Schools are set up for education rather than childcare; it can be more of an institutional than a homely atmosphere.	
You are not constrained by the shorter school day and can work or attend a course.		There is no flexibility – your children have to be picked up when the session or day ends.	
After-school and holiday clubs can introduce children to a range of new activities and hobbies or allow them to spend more time doing a hobby they particularly enjoy.		If a holiday club is held in their school, children can spend the vast majority of their time in a school environment.	
They take care of the transfer from club to school and, in doing so, provide continuous care.		You may have to take time off work to fulfil your contribution to the school club.	
Homework may be completed at the club, so your children can relax once they get home.		You have less idea of your children's progress at school if you are not involved in their homework.	

In-home childcare

Friends and relatives

If you have a ready and willing friend or relative this can be a more economical form of childcare that also offers flexibility and peace of mind.

> *'The thought and care that my mum put in far surpassed what hired help would have given. She was doing it for her grandchildren and was developing the next generation.'*

Friends or relatives may look after your child in your home, their own home or a combination of both. This may be called informal childcare, but you should bear in mind that it is still a form of childcare, and although not all the same rules apply, effort is needed to make it work well.

> *'When using family for childcare, I spent a lot more time worrying about the situation, and found it incredibly time consuming managing the relationship.'*

You may decide to use other forms of childcare, but use friends or a relative to help out either on a regular or ad hoc basis. To benefit from assistance from the Government such as Tax Credits you have to use registered childcare. In order for you to qualify for this, your friend or relative would have to become a registered childminder or nanny. For further details see page 178.

Suitable for:

- Those who can't afford or would rather not use other types of childcare and have willing friends or relatives near by.
- Those who have a friend who wants company for their young child.
- Ad hoc childcare or out-of-school and holiday care.
- Care of a young baby. This may not be suitable as your child grows older, as full-time care for toddlers can be quite draining!

Friends and relatives pros	✓	Friends and relatives cons	✗
They truly have your children's best interest at heart.		Your children may not get as many opportunities to socialise with children of a similar age.	
Usually a cheaper or free form of childcare.		Theye may not be able to accommodate the hours you want – they have their own life too.	
They can probably still care for your children if they are ill.		In order for you to qualify for any financial assistance from the Government, a friend will have to become a registered childminder or nanny. A relative will have to become a registered childminder.	
Your children have the opportunity to form a very close and lasting bond with your relative or friend.		You may not have the same ideas on childrearing issues; you may feel they are too soft or too strict – and it can be harder to raise and deal with issues with those you are close to.	
Your children are looked after in a home setting – reassuring for young children.		They are unlikely to take holidays at the same time as you.	
They may be happy to do school or activity-group pick-up and drop-off and after-school care.		There may not be a guaranteed back-up if they are ill.	
You and your children know the carer very well already.		You may feel indebted and unable to ask for greater flexibility or more hours.	
Your children will receive lots of individual attention.		Your children may reach some educational milestones later as the early years curriculum is unlikely to be followed.	
Your children can stick to their own routines and changes can be made according to their needs.		They may not have the energy to run around after a toddler (and ensure they are safe) all the time.	
Your children are less likely to pick up minor illnesses from other children.		You may not feel their home is as safe or clean as yours.	

Friends and relatives pros	✓	Friends and relatives cons	✗
They may be able to help with additional childcare if there is a change of plan or a crisis and also offer a degree of flexibility to suit your working hours.		You are likely to feel responsible for them as well as your child.	
They are likely to be parents or grandparents themselves, and therefore to have seen it all before.		If they are looking after their own child at the same time they may give preferential treatment.	
They are probably able to help all year round.		If you have a serious disagreement you may be affecting a fundamental relationship in your and your children's life.	
Your money can go to people you care about, or if you are not paying, you can provide payment in kind.		If your mother is looking after your children, your father may start to feel neglected! Or the other set of grandparents may feel left out.	

Nannies, maternity nurses and night nannies

Nannies

Nannies usually look after your children in your home. They are usually given sole charge, for some if not all of the time. Their duties tend to relate solely to looking after the children in their care; these are often referred to as 'nursery duties':

- Planning and preparing children's meals and babies' feeds.
- Dressing and washing of children.
- Caring for and playing with children.
- Washing and ironing their clothes.
- Keeping child-related areas clean: kitchen, playrooms, bed and bathrooms.

Importantly, nannies take full responsibility for the children in their care. They work hard to ensure their safety at all times. They should also help the children to develop key skills and abilities in line with their developmental milestones.

Suitable for:

- Parents who need a long period of cover during the day, or early morning or late evening cover.
- Parents who have one or more children under school age.

- Parents with twins, triplets or more ...
- Parents who would rather have in-home than out-of-home care.

Nanny pros	✓	Nanny cons	✗
On the whole they are well qualified and/or experienced.		Nannies look after your children unsupervised and there is no national register.	
You can leave them in sole charge.		As a rule, nannies only attend to nursery duties.	
This tends to be a more professional relationship than with other in-home childcarers. You can feel less responsibility for them.		Depending on the number of children you have, this can be the most expensive option.	
You can often mould the job and their hours to suit your needs.		Some nannies can be less flexible in terms of hours and when they work than other forms of in-home childcare.	
A well-trained, newly qualified nanny can be a less expensive option than a nanny with more experience, particularly if you want to give sole charge only part of the time.		Newly qualified nannies may need some hand-holding at the beginning and need some time to get up to speed.	

Further information on nanny shares, part-time nannies, nanny housekeepers and male nannies can be found in Chapter 10 (see page 133).

Maternity nurses

Maternity nurses usually provide 24-hour live-in care for the first few weeks of your baby's life. They can take sole charge of a newborn, but normally work alongside the mother. They help to settle the baby into a routine that works for the family and its lifestyle. Importantly, they help to get the baby to sleep through the night or for a large part of the night – they normally sleep in the same room as the baby. They will advise on all aspects of newborn care from feeding to hygiene, and sleep routine to health concerns.

As well as helping the baby sleep, their job is to allow parents to rest and recuperate after the birth and therefore enjoy their baby. They should not be expected to act as a nanny to your other children, but they should interact with them quite happily and be ready to lend a helping hand in a crisis! They are usually found through agencies or by word of mouth.

Suitable for:

- Parents with a newborn baby … or newborn twins or triplets!

Maternity nurse pros	✓	Maternity nurse cons	✗
Round-the-clock, professional care for the first few weeks.		Probably the most expensive form of childcare.	
Establishes your baby in that all-important sleep routine.		You may feel they are more intimate than you with your newborn and this may affect your bonding process.	
Peace of mind; advice and experience on tap.		Can create a sense of dependency or an inability to cope.	
Ensures you get precious sleep in the early weeks.		Can give a false sense of security.	
Helps you through the low points.		Has to be booked weeks or months in advance to coincide with your due date.	
Very helpful if you have twins or triplets.		They may have very set views on childcare which do not coincide with yours.	
Can help with older siblings if negotiated in advance.		You have to pay even if the baby puts in a late appearance.	

Night nannies

A night nanny is usually a qualified nanny who will stay overnight and take sole charge and then leave in the morning. The benefits can be two-fold: you have an uninterrupted night's sleep and while you are happily in the land of nod, an expert is working at getting your child into a good sleep routine. You can employ a night nanny for anything from a single night to three months.

You may like to use one for a special occasion, such as an anniversary, to have the luxury of a long morning lie-in, or in order to stay away from home altogether.

Suitable for:

- Parents with newborn babies or with an older child who is not sleeping well.
- Parents who have to be away overnight for business or a holiday.

Night nanny pros	✓	Night nanny cons	✗
Peace of mind; advice and experience on tap.		They can be expensive.	
Establishes your baby in that all-important sleep routine.		Can give you a false sense of security.	
You get a good night's sleep or a night away.		Can create a sense of dependency or an inability to cope.	
You have your house to yourself or your usual routine/childcare during the day.		There can be a lack of continuity; you may not get the same nanny each time.	
Very helpful if you have twins or triplets.		They may have set views on childcare which do not coincide with yours.	
Flexibility; they can be used for just one night, or a certain number of nights a week.		You may not enjoy having someone in your house overnight and feel you have a lack of privacy.	
They can be booked quickly or in an emergency.		There may not be a night nanny service or agency in your area.	

Au pairs and mother's helps

Au pair

An au pair is probably the cheapest in-home childcare option, but is also the one that can require the most management and guidance. An au pair role is not a job but a cultural exchange. In return for board, lodging, pocket money and the chance to experience a different culture and improve their English, young people (usually between 18 and 30) from abroad help with childcare and light housework. The majority stay for a few months or a year; some stay for longer. If they come from the EU they do not need a visa, but are likely to do so if they come from elsewhere. They will expect to be given time off to attend language classes. If their visa allows it, they may supplement their income through other work such as bar work and babysitting. The Home Office guidelines state that you should not leave an au pair in sole charge of children under 3 years of age, although this is left to your discretion.

Traditionally, au pairs have tended to be female, but there are now an increasing number of male au pairs – a great option if you have energetic boys!

> 'He was great with the boys and always playing sport but I also had to deal with a 20-year-old bloke with smelly feet and an untidy manner.'

Au pair plus

The surge in au-pair-finding websites and the opening of EU borders has meant an increasing number of people now offer themselves as an au pair plus. Similar in principle to an au pair, they tend to have more relevant experience and can work longer hours than an au pair. They may already have good English or be from an English-speaking country, for example, the USA, Australia or South Africa. They may stay longer than an au pair as they are receiving more money. If they are interested in working with children, it can be a good stepping stone towards becoming a nanny. As they are unlikely to be qualified to begin with, you should certainly put them in the bracket of mother's helps, rather than nannies.

Au pair couple

This is becoming an increasingly common option, but you do need to have a big enough room or a separate flat or cottage for the couple. Generally, the female fulfils the au pair role and the male does odd jobs and gardening for you and/or finds a job locally. An au pair couple brings twice as many skills and is more independent, as they have each other. If you have a large family you may want two au pairs to carry out the traditional au pair role. You may like to employ a traditional male/female couple or two au pairs either male or female; it may help if they are friends already, although this can be hard to find.

Au pairs are suitable for:

- Parents who need a helping hand as the size of their family increases.
- Parents whose children are past the baby stage and who are happy to leave their au pair or mother's help in sole charge from time to time.
- Parents who work from home and so can keep a close eye on things.
- Parents who need extra help in the school holidays (students look for au pair or mother's help positions during the university and college holidays).
- Those who have a suitable extra bedroom (for a live-in au pair or mother's help) – they should not have to share with the children and should have room and facilities to study.

An au pair or mother's help is not suitable as a full-time sole charge childcare option, particularly if you have younger children.

> *'It is like having another child, which sometimes can be a real pain but at other times is a real bonus because they enjoy having lots of fun with the children.'*

Au pair pros	✓	Au pair cons	✗
One of the cheapest childcare options.		They can be very reliant on you and your family. You may feel responsible for them and homesickness can be a problem.	
No tax or National Insurance to contend with, unless you are paying more than £100 per week.		They may have very little childcare experience.	
They are often in their late teens or early twenties which means they have lots of energy to help your children burn off their energy!		They should not be left in sole charge of newborn babies or very young children.	
They will help with housework as well as with childcare.		It can sometimes be hard to gauge the authenticity of references.	
If they are in agreement, they can offer flexibility as to when they work.		They can lack maturity and you may feel it is like having another child in your home.	
With an in-built babysitter you can be more spontaneous with your social life.		You are unlikely to meet your new au pair before she arrives to live in your home.	
They can be hired with additional skills, for example, musical, artistic, horse-riding.		Due to visa restrictions, they may only be able to stay a year.	
Your children can learn about different cultures and languages.		A lack of good English could be dangerous in an emergency and they may not know first-aid basics.	
They can provide overnight cover if your children are old enough.		They may find it hard to discipline children.	
They are normally keen to accompany you on holiday.		Depending on their upbringing, they may have done very little housework.	
A couple will be less dependent on you and your family.		An au pair couple needs a bigger living space and some people object to the idea of another man around their home and children.	

Au pair pros	✓	Au pair cons	✗
More au pairs are choosing this as a way of life for a few years. You can find some very experienced and genuine people at a very reasonable cost.		Unless you are employing an au pair plus, your au pair may well need set times off to attend classes.	
You can teach them how to look after your house/children exactly as you would like.		They can need constant management and can be less likely to work under their own initiative.	

Mother's help

Mother's helps are usually unqualified childcarers who have relevant experience or are keen to gain experience. They may be studying childcare and working to supplement their studies. They may be from this country or from elsewhere. This can be a great option if you want an extra pair of hands. As well as helping to lighten the load, they can get things done while you spend time with the children or take them to their activities. Having gained enough experience, some mother's helps go on to be nannies.

See page 63 for the list of circumstances in which an au pair or mother's help is suitable.

Mother's help pros	✓	Mother's help cons	✗
Will help with housework as well as childcare.		Unlikely to have childcare qualifications.	
Cheaper than a nanny.		May not know first-aid basics.	
A mother's help may have had children herself so can be very experienced or may want to be a nanny and be very keen to learn.		Depending on experience, they should not be left in sole charge or only for short periods of time (particularly with young children).	
Can work well if your children are school aged.		A younger mother's help may not stay for a very long time.	
May be happy to accompany you on holiday.		If from abroad, they may be very reliant on you and your family. You may feel responsible for them and homesickness can be a problem.	
May provide overnight cover if your children are old enough.		If they are coming from abroad, you might not meet them until they start work for you.	

Combining different options

With the Government doing more and more to ensure good quality childcare for all, there are an increasing number of options. Consequently, parents are doing more mixing and matching of childcare. You do not need to decide on one form of childcare and stick to it; you can plan a solution with two or more options to suit your needs, those of your children and your budget.

For example, you may find that a childminder is the cheapest option but not want your children to have a long day away from home. A combination of a nanny and childminder may therefore be most suitable for you until your children are a bit older. Or your sister may offer to help out one day a week; taking her up on this offer could be a good option for your sister, your children and your bank account.

- **Pick-ups and drop-offs:** Many forms of childcare offer to pick your children up or drop them off with another form of childcare, so you do not necessarily need to be there for the transition.
- **The impact on your children:** Don't worry about using different kinds of childcare. Children are adaptable, but they also like routine and like to know what to expect. You could use two or three different types of childcare during the week but should try to keep it as a constant from week to week. For example, they could spend two days a week with Granny, three mornings a week at pre-school and the rest of the time at a day nursery.
- **Five days a week:** If you want to spend time at home with your children, do not feel that you need to employ a full-time childcarer. A childminder, nanny or nursery should be quite happy for you to use them three or four days a week.

The Government and childcare

There is an enormous amount of Government interest and investment in childcare and early years education, as outlined in the Department for Children, Schools and Families Children's Plan. The Government is working to provide affordable, flexible, high-quality childcare places for all children. In your search for childcare you may come across the following areas and terms.

Sure Start

This is a Government programme designed to give a great start in life to every child in the UK. It aims to help children, families and communities by increasing the availability of good quality childcare for all by improving the health and emotional development of children and by supporting parents towards employment. Each region (England, Northern Ireland, Scotland and Wales) is responsible for its own programme so there are differences from area to area. In Wales, the Sure Start programme has been amalgamated into Cymorth (the Children and Youth Support Fund).

Every Child Matters

Under Sure Start, in some regions of the UK, is the Every Child Matters initiative. This aims to improve the outcomes for all children in the following areas:

- Being healthy.
- Staying safe.
- Enjoying and achieving through learning.
- Making a positive contribution to society.
- Achieving economic well-being.

Early years curriculum

Each region in the UK also has its own early years curriculum. All children over the age of 3, attending Government-registered settings that deliver the early years curriculum, are eligible for five free early years funding sessions per week for up to 38 weeks during the year. (See page 178 for further details.)

In England, all schools and Ofsted-registered childcarers must take children through the early years foundation stage curriculum until the end of the academic year in which a child has its fifth birthday. This replaces the Curriculum Guidance for the Foundation Stage, the Birth to Three Matters framework and the National Standards for Under 8s Day Care and Childminding.

Settings must ensure every child has an enjoyable and challenging learning and development experience tailored to their needs. Written summaries of the child's progress must be compiled against the six early learning goals. These are:

- Personal, Social and Emotional Development.
- Communication, Language and Literacy.
- Problem Solving, Reasoning and Numeracy.
- Knowledge and Understanding of the World.
- Physical Development.
- Creative Development.

For more information see everychildmatters.gov.uk.

In Scotland, the curriculum is split into two parts, with the first part, Birth to Three, supporting younger children. The second part is known as

A Curriculum Framework for Children 3 to 5. It will be replaced by the Curriculum for Excellence for Children 3 to 6 during 2009 and 2010. For more information see the Learning and Teaching Scotland site (ltscotland.org.uk).

In Wales, the early years curriculum is known as the Foundation Phase, which is designed for children between 3 and 7 years of age. Further details can be found on the Welsh Assembly Government sites (accac.org.uk and wales.gov.uk).

In Northern Ireland, schools have to follow the Curricular Guidance for Pre-school Education which is in line with the Pre-school Education Expansion Programme. For more information go to the Department of Education for Northern Ireland site (deni.gov.uk).

Sure Start Children's Centres
A key part of the Government's strategy are the Sure Start Children's Centres. These aim to be a key feature within each community for parents and carers of children up to the age of 5. They offer a wide range of support: midwives, health visitors, day care, early years education as well as support and skills training for parents.

The Childcare Register

The 2006 Childcare Act introduced the Childcare Register, which has a compulsory and a voluntary part:

The Compulsory Childcare Register
All out-of-home childcare and early education settings such as childminders, day and work nurseries, crèches, nursery schools and pre-schools are regularly inspected by the Government. This ensures that the provider is delivering on all necessary elements including, where appropriate, the early years curriculum. You should not use a provider that is not Government registered. In England and Wales, the latest inspection reports can be viewed online at ofsted.gov.uk under Inspection Reports.

The Voluntary Childcare Register
The voluntary register enables childcarers who are not eligible for compulsory registration to become Government registered. Generally, this covers nannies working in people's homes and those looking after children who are 8 years or over. As well as ensuring good standards of care, it also enables parents to gain additional financial support (see Chapter 12 for more details). This replaces the Childcare Approval Scheme. For more information go to ofsted.gov.uk or call 08456 404040.

CHAPTER 4

Deciding What You Need

Making the right childcare decision can make such a difference to your life. The peace of mind that you feel once your children are happy, settled and well looked after is priceless – and it also allows you to get on with what you need to do.

However, as many have found through a fraught or traumatic experience, making a rushed or panicked childcare decision can actually make your life more difficult.

Whether you are at one end of the spectrum, looking for cover to return to work full time, or at the other end, needing an extra pair of hands, with absolutely no intention of ever setting foot in an office again, you need to give the area of childcare proper thought and consideration. This process should reduce your decision to a smaller one with a clear path and direction. This chapter will take you through the necessary steps to help you make the right choice for your child and yourself.

Your needs

To help you make your choice you should identify your three or four key criteria. This will help you in the two main parts of your childcare quest:

- To decide which type of childcare best suits you.
- To make your final decision and decide from a shortlist which place or person best suits your child.

You will already be formulating your thoughts having looked through the different options in the previous chapter. Before making any final decisions, work through the following headings, which pose a number of questions for you to think about. Write your needs for each in the space provided. Then write and rank your criteria in order of importance in the table provided (see page 73).

When

- For what hours do you need childcare: full time, part time or occasional?
- If part time, is this full days or half days?
- What specific hours would you prefer?

For example: *Three days a week, Monday, Tuesday and Thursday, 8.30am–5.30pm.*

Your needs:

For whom – your children

- How many children do you have and what are their ages?
- Do they have any special needs or illnesses?
- Do they have any particular worries or issues, for example, a very shy child, a particularly difficult child?
- Would being in a large group have an impact on them? Would being at home on their own with a childcarer pose any problems?

For example: *Two children aged 3 and 18 months. The older can be quite demanding.*

Your needs:

Where – your location

- Does your location present any problems, for example, is it very rural?
- If working, do you need to travel far? Will you need to drop off close to a station/bus stop?
- Will the need to park when dropping off the children be a potential problem?

- What is available in your area?

For example: *In London, so parking and competition for good nurseries/childminders could be a problem. Better if I can drop off on way to work.*

> **Your needs:**

Your budget

- How tight is your budget?
- Is there anything that could help spread the money further, for example, a spare room or separate flat that live-in help could use, or a relative who could help out one day a week?

For example: *Money is very tight, having just bought house, so need to weigh up all the options carefully. Could potentially use spare room for live-in help.*

> **Your needs:**

Flexibility/other ideas

- What is your flexibility in terms of days or timekeeping?
- What will be the contribution of your partner/friends/relatives?
- Are there any options for nanny sharing or sharing lifts? Will you need someone to drop children off at school or activities?

For example: *Little flexibility in terms of my job. A friend has talked of a possible nanny share.*

> **Your needs:**

Long term

- What are your long-term needs or plans?
- Are you looking for something for the long term or will your children be starting school soon? If so, will you need holiday cover?
- Are you likely to have another child soon? If so, what is the impact likely to be?

For example: *Considering a third child but not definite, so just need to find what is best for right now.*

Your needs:

You

- What are your feelings about childcare? How do you feel about having someone else in your home? How do you feel about your children spending long hours in a nursery?
- Would you prefer your children to have lots of fun or to be learning as well?
- What did the questionnaire in Chapter 1 tell you about your attitude to parenting and childcare?

For example: *Rather not have someone in my home but if it is the cheaper option we may have to. Want well-qualified and reputable childcare.*

Your needs:

Your criteria

Now transfer your needs in order of importance into the table below. Mark with a star those it is vital that your childcare fulfils. These are your key criteria.

For example:

Ranking	Area	Your criteria
1*	Budget	Must be as cost effective as possible (but good quality).
2*	Location	Ideally on way to work, with parking.
3*	Children	Need someone who can be very loving, but firm with a 3-year-old.
4*	When	Must be able to do three full days: Monday, Tuesday and Thursday.
5	Other ideas	Worth asking my friend about nanny share.
6	Me	Rather not have live-in childcare, but may have to.
7	Long term	No impact at the moment.

Ranking	Area	Your criteria
1		
2		
3		
4		
5		
6		
7		

Linking criteria to childcare choice

Armed with your criteria, return to the main childcare choices in Chapter 3 that appealed to you. Work through them again, and add further ticks or crosses in light of your criteria.

Which ones can you now delete? If there are two or three you still can't decide between, have a look at which has the most ticks or crosses. Also listen to your heart – which feels right for you and your child. Sometimes it is worth paying that little bit more for your peace of mind. You may well decide there are two different avenues you want to investigate at the same time, before making a final decision. You may choose to use a combination of two types of childcare so your children get the benefits from both.

> *'We weren't sure if a nursery was the best option, but decided to try it out and if it didn't work, it didn't work.'*

If you are still struggling, use the following table to help you think through your dilemmas and discuss things with your partner or a friend. Look at the example below first to show you how to fill in the table.

Choice 1: Nursery	
Key pros and cons	+ *Children will be socialising.* + *Children will be learning in a structured way.* – *Hard enough to get myself up and out in the mornings, let alone two small children!*
Lifestyle impact	• *Mornings will be really hard work.* • *Children will be tired in the evenings.* • *Once they are in nursery I need not worry about them too much.* • *May have to find additional cover if I need to work long hours.*
Budget impact	• *Need to talk to local nurseries and weigh up if it is a cheaper option than a nanny. (Will any do a discount for two children?)*
Other impact and needs	• *Would not lose spare room or privacy.* • *Will not need to manage anyone.*
Your thoughts	• *Worried about quality of affordable nurseries with spaces.*

Choice 2: Nanny

Key pros and cons	+ Nanny provides in-home care. + Lots of one-on-one time. − Nanny is expensive.
Lifestyle impact	• No need to have children up and out by 7.30am. • Could work late when needed. • May be the best option for demanding 3-year-old.
Budget impact	• Two children, so could make sense. • However, could only afford live-in. • A nanny share could bring the cost down.
Other impact and needs	• Will lose spare room and have someone living in the house - husband not going to be that happy!
Your thoughts	• Husband would need to be in agreement. • Slightly worried by thought of managing a nanny.

Actions:

• Find out about local nurseries in terms of availability, costs and standards.

• Talk to husband about live-in nanny.

• Talk to friend about sharing nanny (if she lived with us it would be more affordable).

• Weigh all up against criteria and make that decision!

Choice 1:

Key pros and cons	
Lifestyle impact	
Budget impact	
Other impact and needs	
Your thoughts	

Choice 2:	
Key pros and cons	
Lifestyle impact	
Budget impact	
Other impact and needs	
Your thoughts	

Choice 3:	
Key pros and cons	
Lifestyle impact	
Budget impact	
Other impact and needs	
Your thoughts	

Actions:
•
•
•
•
•
•
•
•

Next steps

Your decision is just about made – well done! As childcare is such an emotive subject just working out what will work best for your family can be a major mission and cause of stress. Now you need to consider the following points in preparation for the next bit ... the search:

- **Clearly define your criteria:** For example, what is your exact budget? How far are you prepared to travel to drop off your children? What are you totally non-negotiable on? Going into your search knowing what you want, and why, will make it easier.
- **Arrange temporary cover if necessary:** You need to work hard on your search. Put non-urgent things aside – good childcare can be the foundation of your family's life, so get those foundations right! Finding temporary cover will help you keep things in perspective and stop you from making a rushed decision – which you may well regret.
- **Ask for recommendations:** Nothing puts your mind at rest more than a personal recommendation. Ask your friends, and others you know with children of similar ages, if they have any recommendations. You should still make all the checks that you normally would.
- **Do not let people change your mind:** Remember that different things work for different people. You have worked out what you think is right for you. People may tell you that you are totally insane for choosing as you have done, but if you think it will work for you, give it a try. You may be surprised to find your friends following suit in a few months' time! Remember that you can get good and bad examples of every type of childcare, so if someone has had a bad experience of one it does not mean that you will. However, do ensure you use any information they give you. Ask them what you could learn or do differently to ensure you do not have a similar problem.

Now you are ready to move on to the appropriate chapter to start searching for your childcare.

Being adaptable

At times, when looking after your children, you may feel stuck in some Groundhog Day nightmare where your life never seems to be moving on to the next stage. At other times you will be amazed by how fast the needs of both you and your children change.

You may have always disliked the idea of a nanny, and have decided to find a childminder. The ensuing search could have found you a superhuman and super-nice childminder in the neighbouring street, whom your child adores – things could not be better! But you never know what is around the corner. She may decide to stop childminding, you may become pregnant with twins whom she is unable to accommodate, the thought of three lots of nursery fees could be rather terrifying, never mind getting three children under the age of 4 up and out in the morning – a nanny may prove to be a cheaper and easier option …

Everyone's needs change over time. You need to be open-minded about different childcare options, and make adjustments and changes when necessary. Human beings generally do not like change, but to help your children you need to be as accepting as you can and encourage them to do the same. If you drag your heels and make a fuss about having to make a change in childcare, it will only make it worse for them … and in turn worse for you.

Part 2

Out-of-home Options

CHAPTER 5

Day Nurseries, Work Nurseries and Crèches

This chapter will take you through each step of finding and working well with a day nursery, work nursery or crèche. There are further details on these options, including their pros and cons, in Chapter 3 (see page 45). This chapter will help you to search, screen, visit and make that final decision.

> *'I think nurseries should be for fun; they will get their education when they start school.'*

The things you want to know first

What you can expect from them

- They will attend to all your child's needs while in their care.
- They will have appropriate equipment and toys.
- They will ensure appropriate structured and stimulating activities to aid development.
- Healthy food is usually provided by nurseries, but with some you may have to pay extra for formula milk and nappies, or supply your own. (A crèche may not supply drinks and snacks.)
- They will follow the appropriate early years curriculum.
- They will monitor, record and report your child's development and achievements.

Hours

- Most day and work nurseries will open for 11 or 12 hours a day, from either 7am or 8am until 6pm or 7pm.
- Crèche opening hours are likely to be more limited, for example, mornings only.

Adult-to-child ratios

- One adult to three children for 0–2-year-olds.
- One adult to four children for 2–4-year-olds.
- One adult to eight children from 3 years and upwards.
- There should be no more than 12 babies in a group, and no more than 26 toddlers or pre-school children in any one group.

Staff qualifications

- Supervisors and managers must have at least a Level 3 childcare qualification.
- Of the remaining staff at least half must have a Level 2 childcare qualification or above. (See page 207 for details of childcare qualifications.)
- At least two staff need to be on duty at all times.

Costs

- Nursery fees vary from approximately £150 to £220 per child per week, depending on location. In central London fees can top £300 per week.
- The cost should decrease as your child gets older due to the change in the adult-to-child ratio.
- Crèche costs will range from approximately £2 to £5 per hour. You can often pay by the half hour.
- See Chapter 12 for details of financial help for which you may be eligible.

Special needs

Many nurseries can take children with special needs, and where possible will ensure they are included in all appropriate activities. You will need to work closely with the staff to help them help your child. Fees may be higher due to the extra time and staff required to ensure the right care.

Local authority nurseries and children centres have dedicated special needs staff.

'They get extra money for special needs children so are always keen to take them. You need to make sure they are truly capable. I think the most important thing is that they know how to get the therapists involved.'

Searching and screening

Before you lift up the phone or wiggle your computer mouse on your quest for that caring and fun-filled nursery, fill in the following grid. This will help you to finalise your criteria and help you think about the characteristics and atmosphere you would like the nursery or crèche to have. An example is given to show you how to enter your information.

When	*Three full days: Monday, Tuesday and Thursday, 8.30am–5.30pm.*
For whom	*A 3-year-old boy and 18-month-old girl.*
Where	*On way to station or close to home with good parking.*
Will need to	*Pick up 3-year-old from pre-school when he starts in three months' time.* *Be able to cater for a child with egg intolerance.*
Other needs	*Similar outlook on discipline, so 3-year-old has consistency if he misbehaves.*
Characteristics and atmosphere	*Cheerful, caring, down to earth and fun but able to discipline. Not too noisy or busy.*

When	
For whom	
Where	
Will need to	
Other needs	
Characteristics and atmosphere	

Searching

You know what you want, so now it is just a matter of finding it. You need to find out about the places in your area and start matching them to your criteria. Good nurseries are often fully booked up, but should operate a waiting list. In some areas people put their child down for a nursery before the child is born. So, once you make the decision that a day nursery is the childcare option for you, it is probably best to start searching straight away. If you don't want your child to start for a few months, your final choice may be happy to hold a place for your child.

Try these ways of looking for a good nursery or crèche close to you:

- Search online through Childcare Link (childcarelink.gov.uk). In Northern Ireland use employersforchildcare.org.
- Ask for a list from your local Children's Information Service. Contact them directly or through Childcare Link (childcarelink.gov.uk or freephone 0800 2346 346). In Northern Ireland contact the Childcare Advice and Information Helpline (freephone/text 0800 028 3008 or via employersforchildcare.org). In Scotland visit scottishchildcare.gov.uk.
- The PreSchools Directory lists day nurseries, nursery schools and pre-schools in your area. See preschooldirectory.co.uk.
- Contact the National Day Nurseries Association (NDNA) via ndna.org.uk or on 01484 407070.
- Speak to your health visitor or local medical practice.
- Search your local information websites and phone book.
- For crèches, ask at local leisure and shopping centres.
- Find out if your employer or college has a nursery or crèche.
- Ask around for a word-of-mouth recommendation.

Screening

Many nurseries and crèches will have their own websites, which may answer quite a few of your initial screening questions. These questions should focus on your top criteria or any worries you have. You should also make a preliminary phone call to ask additional questions and ask for a prospectus or information pack.

> *'Just turn up rather than making an appointment. Some nurseries can really stage manage things when they know parents are going to visit.' – Natalie, nursery manager*

If you like what you are hearing and they have a space for your child (or can put you on a waiting list), you should then make a visit. You should try to visit a few nurseries to ensure you make the choice best suited to your child. Remember that every nursery is different.

Whether you decide just to turn up or to make a scheduled appointment, try to do so at a time when there will be quite a lot of children there – but not during likely drop-off, pick-up or meal times as these will be busy and no one will be able to concentrate on you. You may like to turn up unannounced and have a quick chat, and arrange a further visit if you like what you see.

Visiting and checking

What are your first impressions when you enter the nursery or crèche?

- Does it have a nice atmosphere, and is it relatively calm?
- Are the children happy and busy? Are they interacting well with each other?
- Look at how the staff are interacting with the children. Do they seem genuinely interested and involved with them? Do they seem caring and encouraging?
- Look at how the staff are interacting with each other. Do they seem to work as a team? Do they seem more interested in the children than each other?

> *'Look at how loving they are towards the babies. This can help you assess whether they are there for the love of the job or just for the money.'*

Questions to ask

It is important to have a list of prepared questions. Ask questions about the areas you are interested in, or concerned about. Also think about what sort of atmosphere and daily structure will suit your child best. A reputable nursery or crèche will expect you to ask a lot of questions. Ensure you take notes so that you can compare the different places. Here are some of the more common questions that people ask.

The nursery and the staff
- How long has the nursery or crèche been running?
- What is the maximum number of children you can have, and how often is this reached?
- When was the last inspection? Could I see your inspection report and registration and insurance certificates?
- Could you tell me about your relevant experience and training? And that of the other staff?
- How long do your staff normally stay here for?
- Who will be my child's key worker? What are the key worker's

responsibilities? Could I meet the key worker? (In most nurseries each child is allocated a key worker who is mostly responsible for that child.)

- Who would I speak to if I had a problem?
- Are you a member of any associations? Have you achieved any kite marks for excellence (for example, NDNA's Quality Counts, Investors in People or Investors in Children)?
- Do you have any references from parents? Would you mind if I phoned a parent?
- What provision can you make for a child with special needs? (If this is appropriate to you, also discuss any additional agencies they may have to contact or work with.)

> *'Consistency of staff can be the main problem.'*

Beliefs and principles

- What beliefs or principles does the nursery or crèche adhere to? How do you ensure all staff deliver these?
- What is your discipline policy?
- How do staff deal with tantrums?
- How do you work with parents to ensure consistent discipline?
- How would you deal with a particularly difficult child? Or with a particularly shy child?
- What is the daily routine? How much flexibility is there in this? (Discuss any particular needs your child has, or any worries you have about routines.)

> *'You will get children behaving badly towards each other, it is normal behaviour for young children. Their powers of communication aren't great and it is a way of getting what they want or attention. We are vigilant and work at ensuring they understand how to behave well.' – Jennifer, nursery key worker*

Food and sleep

- Do I need to supply my own bottles and formula milk?
- Do you have provision for storing and heating breast milk?
- What are the meal and snack arrangements? Could I have a look at a weekly menu? How often does this change? (Discuss any special dietary requirements your child has.)
- At what time do the children have their meals/snacks?
- What do you do if children refuse to eat, or drink their milk feed?
- How do you let the parents know how much their child has eaten during the day?
- Could I see where the food and/or bottles are prepared?

- At what time and where do the children sleep? Could I have a look? (Check that this looks inviting and is dimly lit.)
- What do you do if a child is not settling down to sleep?

> *'It is really frustrating if they leave your child to sleep for two or three hours when you have asked that she only sleeps for an hour and a half – you have to deal with the consequences when she won't go to sleep on time in the evening.'*

Activities and development
- How are the different age groups split up? Do the different groups come together at any point during the day?
- What activities would a typical day or week consist of? (Ensure there is enough variety.)
- What types of toys and activities are there for the children inside? And outside? Could I have a look please? (Ensure the toys and equipment are well maintained and are not missing any vital bits! There should be different areas such as a 'home' corner for role play, a quiet area for looking at books, small tables and chairs to sit at for drawing, jigsaws and puzzles, water and/or sand play areas, lots of painting and crafts, trains and cars and construction toys. The outdoor area should be enclosed by a fence at least 1.2m high.)
- What do you find the children particularly enjoy?
- Do you take the children on any outings? If so, where? Are there any extra costs involved?
- How do you monitor a child's progress? How do you share this with the parents?
- What would you do if you were concerned about the development or behaviour of a child?
- Do I have to supply my own nappies?
- How do you like to work with parents when potty training?

> *'I found they used cheap nappies which gave my boys a skin rash. I asked them to swap to another type.'*

Sessions for your child
- How do you settle a child into the nursery?
- Are there a minimum number of sessions a week that a child must attend?
- Which group would you put my child in?
- Will my child be with quite a lot of the same children across the week?
- What notice do I have to give if I wish to change the sessions?
- Discuss your preferred start date and whether they have a place, will hold a place or need to put you on their waiting list.

Safety and hygiene
- What safety precautions do you have in place?
- What additional security precautions do you have in place?
- How many of the staff have first-aid training?
- Have you been involved in an emergency situation with a child? If so, what happened and how did you deal with it?
- Have you had to take a child to hospital and if so, what was the reason?
- Could I have a look at the bathrooms and nappy changing areas, please? (Ensure these are clean and fresh.)

> *'They have a password system as an extra security measure, so if someone else is picking up the children for me I tell the nursery and my friend a password for that day.'*

Holidays
- On which days of the year are you closed?
- How much notice do you need if a child is going on holiday?
- What is your policy on charging when a child is on holiday?
- Do you offer holiday care for older children?

Costs
- Do you have a registration fee or a fee to hold a place?
- What are your hourly, weekly or daily charges?
- Do you have additional charges for late collection?
- How often do you like to be paid? In advance or in arrears, and by what method?
- What are your policies on charging when a child is ill?
- How do you arrange deductions for the fees around the free nursery sessions for 3- and 4-year-olds?
- Do you give reductions for siblings or twins?

> *'For me, the difference it makes having the nursery on the way to work is huge. I went for my second rather than first choice to make it easier getting them to and from the nursery before and after work. I still feel I made the right decision.'*

Tips for your parenting style

Following on from the questionnaire in Chapter 1 (see page 23), here are some tips and ideas for working well with nurseries. You should take note of the points for your stronger style(s), or you may like to read through all of them!

Keep them safe

- Do let them know if you are worried about safety or another issue. They will understand and can then work to put your mind at rest.
- Remember not to prolong the goodbye at drop-off, even if your child seems very upset. It will only upset you both even more. Just give a cheery goodbye. The nursery can tell you how long it took your child to settle when you pick up.
- Give your nursery the necessary information they need but avoid being too prescriptive. Remember that they are experienced. Give them the vital information but let them get on with their job and get to know your child themselves.
- If you are worried about an issue, take some time to think about the most productive way of solving it, rather than racing straight in.

   'Say goodbye and don't linger – you are giving the child mixed messages.' – Kate, nursery key worker

Freedom

- Find a nursery that is relaxed, creative and has lots of outside space.
- Make sure their discipline policy suits you.
- Joining a nursery can be a big change for a child, so ensure you have prepared your child for nursery by explaining what will happen and how much fun they will have.
- Ensure you give enough information at drop-off, for example, if your child has had a bad night's sleep. This will help them to be more understanding towards your child through the day.
- Ensure you deal with issues rather than letting things go. This should help your child to settle in better and feel happier about things.
- Take time to discuss how well your child is settling in and do all you can to make this work as well as possible.

Traditional

- Ensure you are happy with the routine of the nursery, as they are unlikely to make too many changes to suit your child.
- If you feel your child is picking up unwanted behaviour, talk to your child's key worker about what this behaviour is and how you can both deal with it.
- If your child is starting on the early years curriculum, don't compare him or her with others. The children will all be developing at different rates and the nursery will be taking this into account.
- Give the nursery both positive and negative feedback to help them continually improve.

CHAPTER 6

Nursery Schools and Pre-schools

This chapter will take you through each step of finding and working well with a nursery school or pre-school. There are further details on these options, including their pros and cons, in Chapter 3 (see page 45). This chapter will help you to search, screen, visit and make that final decision.

> *'There is absolutely nothing as sweet as their first nursery nativity play.'*

The things you want to know first

What you can expect from them

- They will attend to all your child's needs while in their care.
- They will ensure appropriate, structured and stimulating activities to start your child's education, further aid their development and prepare them for school.
- They will follow the appropriate early years curriculum.
- They will have appropriate equipment and toys.
- They will usually provide healthy lunches and snacks.
- They will monitor, record and report your child's development and achievements.
- Most will prefer your child to be potty-trained. If your child is not trained, you will need to supply your own nappies.

> *'The early years foundation stage has welfare requirements which means we have to give equal status to a child's learning, to how the child feels and how we work with their parents. If a child is not comfortable, he will not learn.' – Lucinda, nursery school head*

Hours

Nursery schools

- Most nursery schools are open from 9am to 3.30pm.
- They offer morning, afternoon and all-day sessions.
- Some may provide extended day provision, for example, 8am to 6pm.
- They are closed for school holidays, including half-terms.

Pre-schools

- Pre-schools offer sessions of 2½ to 4 hours, usually in the mornings. These may be every day or on certain days of the week.
- Some are beginning to offer full-time day care.
- They are closed for school holidays, including half-terms.

Adult-to-child ratios

Nursery schools

- Two adults for every 20 to 26 children aged between 3 and 5 years old.

Pre-schools

- One adult to four children aged between 2 and 3 years old.
- One adult to eight children aged between 3 and 5 years old.
- There are often a higher number of adults present as parents are also involved.

Staff qualifications

- In a nursery school class of 26 children, one member of staff must be a qualified teacher and the other a trained nursery nurse or classroom assistant.
- Pre-school staff may be trained nursery nurses and classroom assistants or in the midst of training. The main teacher must have at least a Level 3 qualification and there is a high likelihood that at least one member of staff will be a qualified teacher. (See page 207 for further details of childcare qualifications.)

> *'We have a consistent staff and we know the children and their personalities. We always make sure that they are happy.' — Ann, pre-school supervisor*

Costs

Nursery schools

- Free if the nursery school is part of the state education system.
- Private nursery fees for full-time attendance can vary from £1000 to over £2000 per term depending on location. However, many children will not attend full-time and early years funding can be claimed on five 2½–3 hour sessions a week if your child is over 3 years of age (see page 178).

Pre-schools

- Costs usually range from £3 to £8 per session (though some can charge up to £25 per session, if they operate more like a nursery school).
- Early years funding is also available for those of the right age (see page 178).

See Chapter 12 (page 177) for details of financial help for which you may be eligible.

Some nursery schools and pre-schools ask that your child wears a uniform, which will incur extra costs.

Special needs

Many nurseries can take children with special needs, and where possible will ensure they are included in all appropriate activities. You will need to work closely with their staff to help them help your child. Fees may be higher due to the extra time and staff needed to ensure the right care.

If your child has special needs, you may like to consider a Montessori nursery. The Montessori method was developed through work with special needs children and the individual approach it takes helps children to develop at their own rate and ensure maximum achievement. An additional benefit is that a child normally stays with the same teacher rather than moving up to another class in their second year of nursery. It can be particularly beneficial for needs on the autistic spectrum including Autism, Asperger's Syndrome and Semantic Pragmatic Disorder.

If a nursery school or pre-school is attached to a primary school there may be facilities that your special needs child can use, for example, a sensory room. There may also be additional qualified and experienced staff.

> *'Our pre-school was linked to the primary school. The transition for our son was almost seamless and not at all stressful.'*

Searching and screening

A momentous moment is approaching – you are taking the first steps towards your child beginning formal education. Many parents feel that their children are ready for this stage as they are very keen to learn – and yet they are so young!

You may be of the view that this stage is crucial as it will lay the foundations of your child's entire education, or, you may feel that as long as your child enjoys it, you are quite relaxed about how much, or little, he or she learns. Whatever you believe, it is important that you find a nursery school or pre-school that suits your child and what you feel your child needs.

In order to finalise your criteria and help you think about the characteristics and atmosphere you would like the nursery school or pre-school to have, fill in the grid below. An example is given to show you how to enter your information.

When	Three mornings a week: Monday, Tuesday and Thursday.
For whom	Energetic and spirited 3-year-old boy.
Where	On way to station for me, and close to childminder so she can pick him up afterwards.
Will need to	Allow the childminder to collect him. Be able to cater for a child with egg intolerance. Have similar outlook on discipline, so he has consistency if he misbehaves. Have good outside space to use up his energy.
Additional characteristics and atmosphere	Fun and cheerful, but with a diligent and encouraging approach to education. Need him to enjoy and look forward to going, but also to learn to sit and concentrate for more than five seconds at a time!

When	
For whom	
Where	
Will need to	
Additional characteristics and atmosphere	

Searching

Now you have a clear idea of what you want, you need to find out about the nursery schools and pre-schools in your area and start matching them to your needs. Good nursery schools and pre-schools are often fully booked up, but they should operate a waiting list. In some areas people put their child down for a nursery school before they are born. So, depending on the demand in your area, you should start looking as soon as you decide you want to send your child to one.

Here are some of the main ways of looking for a good nursery school or pre-school close to you:

- Search online through Childcare Link (childcarelink.gov.uk). In Northern Ireland use employersforchildcare.org.
- The Pre-Schools Directory lists nursery schools and pre-schools in your area (preschooldirectory.co.uk).
- Ask for a list from your local Children's Information Service. Contact them directly or through Childcare Link (childcarelink.gov.uk or freephone 0800 2346 346). They can also advise you about wrap-around care (see Chapter 8, page 113). In Northern Ireland contact the Childcare Advice and Information Helpline (freephone/text 0800 028 3008 or via employersforchildcare.org). In Scotland visit scottishchildcare.gov.uk.
- Your local EYDCP (Early Years Development and Childcare Partnership) should also be able to give you details of pre-schools in your area. You should be able to find the details of your EYDCP on your local County Council website.
- The Independent Schools Council provides information about private nursery schools in your area. Contact them on 0845 7246657 or via isc.co.uk.
- For more information on the Montessori method and to search for schools in your area visit montessorieducationuk.org.
- Speak to your health visitor or local medical practice.
- Search your local information websites, phone book and community notice boards.
- Ask around for a word-of-mouth recommendation.

    'They are so proud to be going to "school". It is both sweet and heart-breaking at the same time.'

Screening

Nursery schools

Most nursery schools have their own websites which may answer quite a few of your initial screening questions. These questions should focus on your top criteria or any worries you have. You should also make a preliminary phone call to ask additional questions and to ask for a prospectus or information pack to be sent to you.

If you like what you are hearing and they have a space for your child (or can put you on a waiting list), you should then make a visit. You should try to visit a few nurseries to ensure you choose the one best suited to your child.

Pre-schools

As these are community based and run on a not-for-profit basis, they are less likely to have a website. If this is the case, start with a phone call and ask some basic screening questions. Again, if you like what you hear, ask them to send you an information pack and arrange a visit.

Visiting and checking

First impressions are important. How do you feel when you enter the nursery school or pre-school?

- Does it have a nice atmosphere, and is it relatively calm?
- Are the children happy and busy? Are they interacting well with each other?
- Look at how the staff are interacting with the children. Do they seem caring and encouraging?
- Look at how the staff are interacting with each other. Do they seem to work as a team? Do they seem more interested in the children than each other?

> *'Has your child been welcomed? Does the teacher take an interest in your child or just talk to you? Do they talk about the whole welfare of your child, not just the education?' – Lucinda, nursery school head*

Nursery school and pre-school questions

It is important to have a list of prepared questions. Ask questions about the areas you are interested in, or concerned about. Also think about what sort of atmosphere and daily structure will suit your child best. A reputable nursery school or pre-school will expect you to ask a lot of questions. Ensure you take notes so that you can compare the different schools. Here are some of the more common questions that people ask.

The school and the staff

- How long has the nursery school or pre-school been running?
- What is the maximum number of children you can have, and how often is this reached?
- When was the last inspection? Could I see your inspection report and registration and insurance certificates?
- Could you tell me about your relevant experience or training? And that of the other staff?
- How long do your staff normally stay here for?
- Are you a member of any associations? Have you achieved any kite marks for excellence?
- Who would be my child's teacher and classroom assistant? Could I meet them?
- Who would I speak to if I had a problem?
- What provision can you make for a child with special needs? (If this is appropriate to you, also discuss any additional agencies they may have to contact or work with.)
- Do you have any references from parents? Would you mind if I phoned a parent?

Beliefs and principles

- What beliefs or principles does the nursery or pre-school adhere to? How do you ensure all your staff deliver these?
- What is your discipline policy?
- How do you deal with tantrums?
- How do you work with parents to ensure consistent discipline?
- How would you deal with a particularly difficult child? Or with a particularly shy child?
- What is the daily routine? (Discuss any particular needs your child has, or any worries you have about routines.)
- How do you settle a child into the school? What do you do if a child is not settling well?

> *'We explain our expectations to the children — we have high standards of caring for each other, we are a group, we share and are considerate.' — Ann, pre-school supervisor*

Food and rest

- What are the meal and snack arrangements? Could I have a look at a weekly menu? How often does this change? (Discuss any special dietary requirements your child has.)
- At what time do the children have their meals and snacks?
- What do you do if a child refuses to eat?
- How do you let the parents know how much their child has eaten during the day?
- Do the children have a quiet period after lunch? (If necessary, ask if they have provision for your child to have a short nap.)

Activities and development

- How are the different age groups split up? Do the different groups come together at any point during the day?
- What activities would a typical day or week consist of? (Ensure there is enough variety.)
- In terms of their early education, what do you work towards the children achieving in their first year here? And in their second?
- What types of toys, equipment and activities are there for the children inside? And outside? Could I have a look, please? (Ensure the toys and equipment are well maintained and are not missing any vital bits! There should be different areas such as a 'home' corner for role play, small tables and chairs to sit at for drawing, jigsaws and puzzles, water and/or sand play areas, painting and crafts, trains and cars, construction toys and books within a quiet area. The outdoor area must be enclosed by a fence at least 1.2m high.)
- What do you find the children particularly enjoy?
- Do you take the children on any outings? If so, where? Are there extra costs involved?
- How do you monitor a child's progress? How do you share this with the parents?
- What would you do if you were concerned about the development or behaviour of a child?
- What if my child is not really interested in learning?

> *'We let children choose what they want to do — it helps to develop their confidence. Their eyes are usually out on stalks when they start, as there are so many things to explore!' — Ann, pre-school supervisor*

Sessions for your child

- Are there a minimum number of sessions a week that a child must attend?
- Which group or class would you put my child in?
- Will my child be with quite a lot of the same children across the week?
- What notice do I have to give if I wish to change the sessions?

> *'Look to see if the children are allowed to choose and use their own ideas and are not too directed.' – Lucinda, nursery school head*

Safety and hygiene

- What safety precautions do you have in place?
- What additional security precautions do you have in place?
- How many of the staff have first-aid training?
- Have you been involved in an emergency situation with a child? If so, what happened and how did you deal with it?
- Have you had to take a child to hospital and if so, what was the reason?
- Could I have a look at the bathrooms, please? (Ensure these are clean and fresh.)

Holidays

- Is there a limit to how much time a child can take out for holidays?
- How much notice do you need if a child is going on holiday?

Costs

- Do you have a registration fee or a fee to hold a place?
- What are your hourly, weekly or daily charges?
- How often do you like to be paid? In advance or in arrears, and by what method?
- What are your policies on charging when a child is ill or on holiday?
- How do you arrange deductions around the free nursery sessions for 3- and 4-year-olds?
- Do you give reductions for siblings or twins?

Pre-school only

- I understand I may have to help run some of the sessions. How does this work?
- What would you want me to do and how often?
- What if I am unable to do the sessions?

> *'It is very special when someone's mum comes in to help with a session. Their child is always very excited.' – Ann, pre-school supervisor*

Tips for your parenting style

Following on from the questionnaire in Chapter 1 (see page 23), here are some tips and ideas for dealing with nursery schools and pre-schools. You should take note of the points for your stronger style(s), or you may like to read through all of them!

Keep them safe

- Do not prolong the goodbye at drop-off. Your children are at an age where they need to become more independent. If you react you will only make it harder for them. You want them to enjoy their years at school and a quick, cheery goodbye will help.
- Talk through any worries you have with your child's teacher, for your own peace of mind, but remember they are likely to be well trained not only in child education but also child care.
- Have realistic expectations about the setting – a pre-school may be busy and noisy and a nursery school a bit more formal.
- Make sure you gain confidence in the nursery school or pre-school. The staff are experienced at looking after young children, and although it may feel like a school, they will give them comfort or cuddles as necessary.

   'I advise parents to go on their gut feeling. Use your instincts to assess whether it suits you or not. We can't be all things to all people.' – Lucinda, nursery school head

Freedom

- You may prefer a pre-school or a Montessori nursery school rather than a more traditional nursery school.
- Don't worry about your child having to do too much learning and not having enough fun – all of the learning is done in a fun and relaxed way. However, it is also good preparation for school, for example, they will gradually learn to concentrate for longer periods of time.
- Make sure they don't miss too much school time. While it is not compulsory they attend, you don't want them to feel they are falling behind their peers.
- Ensure the teachers see you dropping your child off so they have a chance to talk to you if they need to.

   'If you are aware that they have had a bad night, you will react to them differently.' – Jennifer, nursery school teacher

Traditional

- Make sure you understand and are happy with the curriculum your child is following.
- Do not be too hard on your child, or expect too much too soon. Remember that your child is still young and much of this will be new to him or her. Your child will have low concentration levels and may also need to build up confidence.
- Don't compare your child with others, as they will all be developing at different rates and the nursery school or pre-school will be taking this into account.
- Ensure you give praise where it is due – the teachers work hard to ensure their charges are learning, but also having fun, and really welcome feedback from the parents.

> *'Parents ask why their children don't know the alphabet or aren't learning to read. They don't always realise how much early learning takes place through play activities. They must have realistic expectations.' – Lucinda, nursery school head*

CHAPTER 7

Childminders

This chapter will take you through each step of finding and working well with a childminder. There are further details on childminders, including their pros and cons, in Chapter 3 (see page 45). This chapter will help you to search, screen, visit and make that final decision.

> *'For me, a childminder is the perfect childcare solution. My son is in a nice home environment, with someone dedicated to his care, and he has a great time playing, doing activities and socialising with a small group of other children – and it is not too expensive!'*

The things you want to know first

What you can expect from them

- They will attend to all your child's needs while in their care.
- They will have suitable toys, games and puzzles to amuse them and aid their development.
- Some will provide meals while others will ask you to supply your own.
- They will let you know if they have any concerns or worries about your child's development.
- From Autumn 2008 all childminders in England and Wales must be able to take your child through the early years curriculum suitable for their age and developmental stage. They will compile a written report of your child's progress.

> *'If your child plays up when you are there, let the childminder keep control, it's her house and her rules' – Becky, childminder*

Hours

- Generally between 8am and 6pm.
- Most can be flexible, although some may be constrained by their own children coming home from school, or the number of children they can look after at a time.
- Most are able to offer part-time care.

Adult-to-child ratios

- One adult to six children (under the age of 8 years).
- Of the six children no more than three of them may be under 5 years old at any one time.
- Of these three children under 5 years, no more than one can be under a year old (this includes their own children if appropriate). Regulating bodies can make exceptions for siblings or twins.

Costs

- Anything between £2.30 and £6 per hour, per child, depending on location and whether the childminder provides meals or other extras.

See Chapter 12 (page 177) for details of financial help for which you may be eligible.

Special needs

Some childminders are experienced in caring for children with specific special needs. Childminding networks can help childminders with extra training in particular areas of special needs.

Childminding groups and networks

Increasingly childminders are joining groups or networks. These provide support for childminders, a forum to share ideas and help in finding back-up cover for holidays or sickness; some also provide access to training.

The National Childminding Association of England and Wales (NCMA), the SMCA in Scotland and the NICMA in Northern Ireland promote quality in registered childminders. One of the main childminding networks is the NCMA-approved Children Come First (CCF), which is also a quality assurance scheme.

Searching and screening

Before you lift up the phone or wiggle your computer mouse on your quest for a loving childminder, try filling in the grid below. This will help you to finalise your criteria and also help you think about the characteristics and atmosphere you would like the childminder and her home to have. An example is given to show you how to enter your information.

When	*Three full days: Monday, Tuesday and Thursday, 8.30am–5.30pm.*
For whom	*A 3-year-old boy and an 18-month-old girl.*
Where	*On way to station or close to home.*
Will need to	*Pick up 3-year-old from pre-school when he starts in three months' time. Have a good amount of outside space.*
Skills needed	*Good with demanding children, safe driver.*
Characteristics and atmosphere	*Cheerful, caring, down to earth and fun but able to discipline. Homely environment but with enough space; not too cluttered and crowded. (See page 209 for a further list of potential childcarer characteristics.)*

When	
For whom	
Where	
Will need to	
Skills needed	
Characteristics and atmosphere	

Searching

You now need to find out who is out there and start matching them to your needs. Good childminders are often fully booked up, but they may operate a waiting list. It is worth putting your name down as a place may come up sooner than expected.

These are some of the main ways of looking for a registered childminder:

- Ask for a list of childminders with vacancies from your local Children's Information Service. Contact them directly or through Childcare Link (childcarelink.gov.uk or on freephone 0800 2346 346). In Northern Ireland speak to your local Health and Social Services Trust – contact the Childcare Advice and Information Helpline (freephone/text 0800 028 3008 or via employersforchildcare.org). In Scotland visit scottishchildcare.gov.uk.
- Contact the National Childminding Association (NCMA) on freephone 0800 169 4486 (10am–4pm Monday to Friday) or via ncma.org.uk. In Scotland contact the SMCA on 01786 445377 or via childminding.org. In Northern Ireland contact the NICMA on 028 9181 1015 or via nicma.org.
- Speak to your health visitor or local medical practice.
- Check community magazines and notice boards.
- Ask around for a word-of-mouth recommendation.

> *'My child often does not want to leave the childminder in the evening, which I can find quite hurtful. However, at least I know she loves it there.'*

Screening

Some childminders have their own website that may answer quite a few of your initial screening questions. These questions should focus on your top criteria or any worries you have. You should also make a preliminary phone call.

If you like what you are hearing and they have a space for your child, or could put your child on a waiting list, you should arrange a visit. Try to arrange a time when there will be children there, but also a time when it will be fairly easy for the childminder to talk to you. Alternatively, organise two visits, a quick one when there are children there and a longer one when there are not.

You should certainly get the childminder to meet your child, either at the first or second meeting.

> *'Don't sweat about the small stuff. Find someone who can have fun with your child. You can't have everything, so work on the priorities for your child's age.'*

Visiting and checking

What are your first impressions when you enter the house?

- Do you like the atmosphere?
- Is the childminder welcoming – and calm?
- Do the children seem to be happy and busy?
- Are you happy with how the childminder interacts with the children?
- If your child is with you, does the childminder take an interest and relate well to him or her?

> *'I was told as a rule of thumb to be wary of those with too clean a house. You want to see toys and activities and know that they are childminding because they love children, not because they want to stay at home to clean their house.'*

Childminder questions

It is important to have a list of prepared questions, rather than thinking of everything you should have asked once you have left. Try to ask questions about the areas you are interested in, or concerned about. Also think about what sort of person will suit your child best. Take notes so that you can compare different childminders. Here are some of the more common questions that people ask.

The childminder

- What do you particularly enjoy about childminding?
- Could you tell me about your relevant experience or training? Are you planning to do any further training in the future?
- Are you a member of any networks or childminding organisations? If so, what do these provide for you?
- Could I see your inspection report and registration and insurance certificates?
- Do you have any references from parents? Would you mind if I phoned a parent?
- How do you like to deal with issues or problems that parents may have?
- What provision can you make for a child with special needs? (If this is appropriate to you, also discuss any additional agencies they may have to contact or work with.)
- Are you happy to deal with a child with allergies? (Discuss any allergies or particular needs your child has.)

'I like providing a family environment, which I feel you don't get in a nursery.' – Becky, childminder

Beliefs and principles

- What beliefs or principles do you adhere to when looking after the children? What do you believe is the secret to a happy and healthy child?
- How do you think children should be disciplined?
- What is your view on tantrums and how to deal with them?
- Have you dealt with a particularly difficult child? Or with a particularly shy child? If so, could you tell me about it and what you did that you think made a difference?
- How do you work with parents to ensure consistent discipline?

  'A childminder may have different values to you; their basic upbringing and character can be very different.'

Adult-to-child ratios

- Tell me about the other children you are looking after? How long have they been with you?
- What is the average number of children you usually have at any one time? Does this include any children of your own?
- How do you juggle things when you are looking after a lot of children at one time?

Food and sleep

- What are your meal and snack arrangements?
- At what time do the children have their meals and snacks?
- What do you do if a child refuses to eat?
- Do you let the parents know how much their child has eaten during the day?
- Do you mind if I have a peek at your kitchen to see where the food is prepared?
- What is the daily routine? How much flexibility is there in this? (Discuss any particular needs your child has, or any worries you have about routines.)
- What are your sleep arrangements? At what time do the other children sleep? Where do they sleep? May I take a look?
- What do you do if a child is not settling down for a rest?

  'As a mother, you have your own standards for your children and no one is ever really going to meet those properly – but you want them to aim pretty high.'

Activities and development

- What activities would you do in a typical day or week?
- Do you provide the early years curriculum once children reach a certain age? If so, how do you manage this with the younger children here as well?
- Do you take the children on outings? If so, where? Are there extra costs involved?
- What types of toys and activities are there for the children inside? And outside? Could I take a look please? (Ensure there is a good selection of toys and activities.)
- What do you find the children particularly enjoy?
- How do you settle a child in and get him or her interacting with the other children?
- How do you monitor a child's progress? How do you share this with the parents?
- What would you do if you were concerned about the development or behaviour of a child?
- How do you like to work with parents when potty training?

> *'Look to see if the childminder gets down on the floor to play with your child when you visit her. It is the child she should be interested in.'*

Hygiene and safety

- What do you do to keep your home safe for the children?
- Have you been involved in an emergency situation with a child? If so, what happened and how did you deal with it?
- If you had to take a child to hospital what would you do with the other children?
- Do you take the children out in the car? What car seats do you have? Are you fully insured for this?
- Do you have any pets?
- Does anyone ever smoke in your home?
- Could I have a look at the bathroom and nappy-changing area, please? (Ensure these are clean and fresh.)

Sessions for your child

- Do you have space at the moment? If not, when do you think you would?
- Are there a minimum number of hours a week that a child must attend?
- Could you do the following days of the week at these times?
- Will my child be with quite a lot of the same children across the week?
- Do you do school pick-ups and drop-offs? If so, from which schools?
- What notice do I have to give if I wish to change the sessions?

> *'Picking up from schools when you have younger children can be difficult. It disrupts sleep and it can be a worry with so many small children and the road.'* – Shelley, childminder

Holidays, illness and back-up childcare

- When do you normally go on holiday?
- How many days illness have you had in the last year?
- Do you have any arrangements for back-up care for holidays and illness?

> *'Hang on, I am not just a childminder, I do have my own life and my own child who needs time.'* – Becky, childminder

Costs

- What are your hourly, weekly or daily charges?
- Do you have additional charges for late collection or agreed extra time?
- How often do you like to be paid? In advance or in arrears, and by what method?
- What are your policies on charging when a child is ill or on holiday?
- Do you give reductions for siblings or twins?

Once you have chosen a childminder, you will need to check her references (see page 180).

Tips for your parenting style

Following on from the questionnaire in Chapter 1 (see page 23), here are some tips and ideas for dealing with childminders. You should take note of the points for your stronger style(s), or you may like to read through all of them!

Keep them safe

- Get to know the childminder, so you are confident in the choice you have made. Any good childminder will understand and take the time to get to know you too.
- Do not prolong the goodbye at drop-off, it will only upset you both even more. If this is the first childcare your child has experienced you do not want him or her to learn that being upset makes you stay longer. For the first couple of days you may like to ask the childminder to text you as soon as your child is settled.
- Ensure you give your childminder the necessary information she needs, and let her know about any worries you have, but do not be too prescriptive; remember she is experienced and well vetted. Give her the vital information but let her get on with her job and get to know your child herself.

> *'I always pass on information, otherwise parents don't have a clue what their child has been doing all day.' – Yvonne, childminder*

Freedom

- Find a childminder who is fun and creative.
- Ensure that you give enough information at handover times, for example, if your child has not eaten much breakfast. It will help both your child and the childminder.
- Ensure you deal with issues, rather than letting things go. This will help your child to settle in better.
- Give plenty of warning if you are going to be late and ensure you pay a bit extra. Do not let it become a habit.
- Remember to manage the boundaries with your childminder. Sharing too much can make it harder to deal with issues.

> *'I love children and I love playing with them.' – Becky, childminder*

Traditional

- Ensure your childminder's routine will work well with yours.
- Talk to your childminder about how you would like your child disciplined and any particular behaviour you would rather not see. You also have to understand that the childminder is coping with quite a few children, and may have to use additional or different rules to make everything run smoothly.
- If the childminder is taking your child through the early years curriculum make sure you understand and are happy with the curriculum they are following and be realistic about what she will help your child to achieve, particularly if she is looking after quite a few children of different ages.
- Always ensure you give praise when it is due – childminding can be quite an isolating job.

   'No clean plate, no pudding. I am also trying to bring up my child in the way that I want.' – Becky, childminder

CHAPTER 8

Out-of-school Care

This chapter will take you through each step of finding the right out-of-school care for your child. There are further details on out-of-school care, including pros and cons, in Chapter 3 (see page 45). This chapter will help you to search, screen, visit and make that final decision.

The things you want to know first

What you can expect from them

- They will attend to all your child's needs while in their care.
- They will ensure appropriate structured, stimulating and restful activities, depending on the time of day.
- They will have appropriate equipment and toys.
- Most will provide appropriate food and snacks, although you may need to provide your own, for some.
- Where necessary, they may escort your child to school and pick them up.

Hours

- Breakfast clubs usually run from 7.30am or 8am until the beginning of the school day.
- After-school clubs run from the end of the school day until 5.30pm or 6pm.
- Holiday-club hours will vary but some will run from 8am to 6pm. Some may open for half-terms as well as the main school holidays. Children can often attend for half days.

   'The holiday club went up to 14 but I think that by the time children were 9 or 10 they would have grown out of it, particularly the girls.'

Adult-to-child ratios

- One adult to eight children aged 3–7 years.
- Children between 8 and 14 may attend, but this must not adversely affect the care of the younger children.
- There must be a minimum of two adults on duty at all times with at least two full staff members in every group of 26 children.

Staff qualifications

- At least half of all staff must hold an appropriate qualification, or be in training to achieve it. This should be at least a Level 2 qualification and supervisors must have a Level 3. (See page 207 for further details of childcare qualifications.)
- All staff should have training in health and safety and child protection policies. At least one staff member with a current first-aid certificate must be on the premises.
- For specialist sporting or adventure activities, the appropriate Government guidelines must be followed.

Costs

These can vary wildly, but some of the clubs linked to schools may be free. Others will charge anything from £2.50 per hour to £7 or more, depending on whether it is community or privately based, if there are pick-ups involved, whether meals or snacks are included and if there are costs associated with the activities. As a rule of thumb, privately provided out-of-school care will cost more. Quite a few clubs offer discounts for siblings.

Special needs

Most out-of-school care provides care for children up to 14; many provide care for special needs children until the age of 16.

Searching and screening

Whatever your reasons for looking for out-of-school care – whether work or studying for a qualification – it is important that you find something that suits your child. Be careful not to plump for the easiest option. If your children do not enjoy their out-of-school care, they could start to associate this with not enjoying school, particularly if they are both on the same premises. With an increasing array of options, you should be able to find something that suits both you and your child.

There are quite a few options available, as most types of childcare offer some sort of out-of-school care. Firstly, think about your children:

- Will they enjoy a noisier atmosphere, with older children, in a breakfast or after-school club?
- Would they prefer the atmosphere of the local nursery, and enjoy being one of the older children there? This might also suit if you have a younger child already there.
- Would they prefer the more homely and calmer setting offered by a childminder?
- Would they rather come straight home after school? (A nanny share, part-time nanny or an au pair would make this possible.)

> *'I don't tend to do structured activities, I checked with the parents and they are happy with this as the children have had a long day.' – Becky, after-school childminder*

In order to finalise your criteria and help you think about the characteristics and atmosphere you would like the facility to have, fill in the grid on page 116. An example is given to show you how to enter your information.

When	Three mornings and afternoons a week: Monday, Tuesday and Thursday.
For whom	An energetic and spirited 4-year-old boy.
Where	Close to or in his new school.
Will need to	Be happy to collect from school. Be able to cater for a child with an egg intolerance. Have good outside space so he can run his energy off.
Additional characteristics and atmosphere	Fun and cheerful, but able to deal with his high spirits. Need him to enjoy and look forward to going, but it must be somewhere that ensures he behaves appropriately.

When	
For whom	
Where	
Will need to	
Additional characteristics and atmosphere	

Now you have a better idea of what you want, you need to find out about the out-of-school care options in your area and start matching them to your needs. Like all childcare, the good ones can become fully booked up very quickly, but they will probably operate a waiting list.

School- and community-based out-of-school care

- Ask for a list from your local Children's Information Service. Contact them directly or through Childcare Link (childcarelink.gov.uk or freephone 0800 2346 346). In Northern Ireland contact the Childcare Advice and Information Helpline (freephone/text 0800 028 3008 or at employersforchildcare.org). In Scotland visit scottishchildcare.gov.uk
- Search online or speak directly to your local Early Years Development and Childcare Partnership (EYDCP) – for their details look on your local County Council website.
- Speak to the local schools and look at flyers, newsletters and information boards at your child's school.
- Search your local information websites, phone book and community notice boards.
- Ask around for a word-of-mouth recommendation.

> *'They are in tears at the beginning of the holiday club because they don't want to leave mum and in tears at the end because they don't want to leave here.' – Anna-Kate, out-of-school and holiday club provider*

The first step is to ensure that the provider is linked to, or able to pick up from and/or drop off at your child's school. Once this is established you should make a preliminary phone call to ask some basic screening questions. These should focus on your top criteria or any worries you have. If you like what you are hearing, ask them to send you an information sheet or pack, if they have one, and arrange a visit.

> *'It is great for my children to get to know other local children who are not at their school.'*

Childminders and day nurseries

For day nurseries see page 84 and for childminders page 106.

Before you decide on one of these options, you will need to establish whether they can drop off at and/or pick up from your child's school. Always visit a few to ensure you make the right choice.

Friends and relatives

A friend or relative who offers out-of-school care may see it as quite an easy favour to perform. However, it is actually a big commitment and you do not want to be left in the lurch if they are unable to help on a certain day. You are advised to approach this in a sensible way and to ensure that the friend or relative can really give you a full commitment. See Chapter 9 (page 125) for more information.

Nanny or au pair

The upside of this arrangement is that your children will not have very long days away from home. They can do their homework, relax or even have friends to play in the security of their own home. Depending on the number of children you have, or if you enter into a part-time nanny share, it may also work out as a fairly economical option. However, you will have to put some effort into managing the relationship. See Chapters 10 and 11 (pages 133 and 159) for more information on nannies, au pairs and mother's helps.

'They have bags of energy as they have been sitting down all day at school. I let them run it off then encourage them to relax.' – Mary, after-school nanny

Visiting and checking

For points to consider when visiting a childminder see page 107, for a day nursery see page 96. If you are visiting a breakfast, after-school or holiday club, make a note of your first impressions and ask yourself the following questions.

- Does the club have a nice atmosphere, and is it relatively calm?
- Are the children happy? Are they interacting well with each other?
- Look at how the staff are interacting with the children. Do they seem caring and encouraging?
- Look at how the staff are interacting with each other. Do they seem to work as a team? Do they also seem more interested in the children than each other? Do they seem to be enjoying what they are doing rather than watching the clock?
- Is the club bright and airy with good and well-maintained equipment?

Out-of-school care questions

It is important to have a list of prepared questions. Try to ask questions about the areas you are interested in, or concerned about. Also think about what sort of atmosphere and structure will suit your child best. A reputable out-of-school facility will expect you to ask a lot of questions. Ensure you take notes so that you can compare the different places. Here are the more common questions that people ask.

The facility and the staff

- How long has the breakfast club/holiday club been running?
- What is the maximum number of children you can have, and how often is this reached?
- When was the last inspection? Could I see your inspection report and registration and insurance certificates?
- Could you tell me about your relevant experience or training? And that of the other staff?
- How long do staff normally stay here for?
- Do you have any references from parents? Would you mind if I phoned a parent?
- How do you transfer children between the club and school? Who does this?
- What provision can you make for a child with special needs? (If this is appropriate to you, also discuss any additional agencies they may have to contact or work with.)

'There were loads of carers so I felt safe leaving them there.'

- Who will be their play worker? Could I meet him or her? How much one-on-one time will my child get? (In most out-of-school clubs each child is allocated a play worker who is mostly responsible for that child.)
- If I had a problem who should I speak to?

Beliefs and principles

- What beliefs or principles does this facility adhere to? How do you ensure all staff deliver these?
- What is your discipline policy?
- How do you work with parents to ensure consistent discipline?
- How would you deal with a particularly difficult child? Or with a particularly shy child?
- What is the daily routine? (Discuss any particular needs your child has, or any worries you have about routines.)

'Children will say, "I am useless, I can't do it." We give them the opportunity to do things they may not get to do during the school day, an opportunity to shine and do something different from their brother or sister. You can really see their self-esteem increase.' — Anna-Kate, out-of-school and holiday club provider

Food and rest

- What are the meal and snack arrangements? Could I have a look at a weekly menu? How often does this change? (Discuss any special dietary requirements your child has.)

- At what time do the children have their snacks and meals?
- What do you do if a child refuses to eat?
- Do you let the parents know how much their child has eaten?
- How do the children rest or relax? Is there a specified quiet area? Do the children have a quiet period after lunch?

> *'There was a drink vending machine there and my children gave me lots of pressure to give them money to buy drinks from it.'*

Activities

- What activities would a typical session or week consist of? (Ensure for holiday clubs that there is enough variety.)
- What types of toys, equipment and activities are there for the children inside? And outside? Could I have a look please? (Ensure the toys and equipment are well maintained and are not missing any vital bits! The outdoor area should be enclosed by a fence at least 1.2m high.)
- What do you find the children particularly enjoy?
- Do you take the children on any outings? If so, where? Are there extra costs involved?
- What do you do about children completing homework? Where is it done and who supervises and helps the children with it?
- If the children are tired after a long day at school, is there somewhere that they can relax? How do you ensure they have down time?

> *'There were so many activities at their holiday club, I thought they would be more exhausted but they seemed to have got the balance about right. I could not have been more pleased with it.'*

Sessions for your child

- How do you settle a child into the sessions? What if my child is not settling well?
- Are there a minimum number of sessions a week that a child must attend?
- Do you separate the younger and older children?
- Will my child be with quite a lot of the same children across the week?
- What notice do I have to give if I wish to change the sessions?

> *'Because they are young, as well as the educational and fun side, it's important to teach and reinforce social skills: respect for each other and waiting their turn are a big part of it. We try not to let the children get too over-excited in the fun games and make sure they know how to calm down for quieter activities.' – Anna-Kate, out-of-school and holiday club provider*

Safety and hygiene

- What safety precautions do you have in place?
- What additional security precautions do you have in place? Do you have a signing-in system?
- How many of the staff have first-aid training?
- Have you been involved in an emergency situation with a child? If so, what happened and how did you deal with it?
- Have you had to take a child to hospital and if so, what was the reason?
- Could I have a look at the bathrooms please? (Ensure these are clean and fresh.)

Costs

- Do you have a registration fee or a fee to hold a place?
- What are your hourly, weekly or daily charges?
- How often do you like to be paid? In advance or in arrears, and by what method?
- What are your policies on charging when a child is ill?
- Do you give reductions for siblings or twins?

Tips for your parenting style

Following on from the questionnaire in Chapter 1 (see page 23), here are some tips and ideas for working with out-of-school care, for each of the styles. You should take note of the points for your stronger style(s), or you may like to read through all of them!

Keep them safe

- Don't hesitate to ask all the questions you want to. You probably will not have attended an out-of-school or holiday club yourself so will not know what to expect. Any good provider will be happy to answer your questions and concerns.
- Don't hover and prolong the goodbye at drop off. You want your children to enjoy their time there and a quick goodbye will help with this and allow them to start getting involved in whatever is going on.
- You may not have much chance to talk to your out-of-school care provider, but if you have any concerns or worries it is important that you talk to them rather than other parents.

> *'Parents know they are safe, and they are learning a language or a new skill at the same time.' — Anna-Kate, out-of-school and holiday club provider*

Freedom

- Make sure you are happy with the kind of activities and routine they are providing, and that you feel your child will have enough time to relax and have fun.
- At drop-off, ensure that you give enough information, for example, if your child has had a bad night's sleep. If your child is going to an after-school club, make arrangements to ensure this information is delivered to the relevant play worker at the end of the school day.
- If dropping off your child yourself, make sure that whoever is in charge knows he or she is there.

> *'They divided them into their age groups and then each group worked its way round all the activities, like arts and crafts, relay games, music.'*

Traditional

- Make sure you are happy with the activities and routine they are following.
- If you would like your child to complete homework at their after-school club, ensure you talk about how this is done.
- If your child is going to a holiday club, ensure you are happy with the discipline, as you may not like to see all your efforts (and those of your child's school) unravel throughout the holidays.
- Ensure your child is not doing back-to-back activities but has time to learn through play and also to relax and unwind.
- Ensure you give praise where it is due – the play workers will be putting in long days and will really welcome feedback from the parents.

> *'I really liked the tennis and the rounders ... oh, and the football.'* – *Tom, 7, attending holiday club*

Part 3

In-home Options

CHAPTER 9

Friends and Relatives

This chapter will take you through the steps to successfully using a friend or a relative for your childcare. There are additional details on using friends and relatives for childcare, including pros and cons, in Chapter 3 (page 45). This chapter will help you to identify and discuss your needs, to decide whether or not to pay and to sort out the formalities that you may need for mutual protection.

The things you want to know first

What you can expect from them

This is up to you and the individual to agree upon, but you will probably expect your friend or relative to:

- Attend to all your child's needs whilst in their care.
- Ensure your child is safe and secure at all times.
- Ensure the day and the activities within it are appropriately structured for your child's age.
- Have appropriate equipment and toys.
- Provide healthy meals and snacks at appropriate times.
- Give you a summary of your child's day and achievements.
- Voice any worries or concerns they have about your child's behaviour or development.

> *'I come home and both my children are so happy and delightful. They are clearly getting what they need out of life and that makes me happier too.'*

Hours and costs

Be sensitive about asking for too many hours, particularly if your friend or relative is very busy or a bit older. Costs vary enormously due to the particular arrangement – from nothing at all to the going rate. If you are not paying or paying very little, ensure that you show your thanks in other ways, for example, by giving thoughtful presents or paying for a night out. If you pay your friend or relative and she applies for registration with the Voluntary Childcare Register, you may be able eligible for Tax Credits from the Government or Childcare Vouchers from your employer (see page 177 for details).

Staff qualifications and adult-to-child ratios

Unless you are paying a friend who has registered as a childminder or nanny, or a relative who has registered as a childminder, qualifications and adult-to-child ratios do not apply.

Special needs

A relative, in particular, will give as much love and care as you do to your child and, if viable, it is likely that you would prefer this option. However, you should carefully consider the needs of both your child and your friend or relative, as it may be a lot to ask. You do not want your child's development, an older relative's health or your relationship with them to suffer. If considering this option, you might like to start off with a trial period of six weeks or two months. You can then review how the arrangement is working and make changes as necessary.

Identifying your needs

Chances are, if you are thinking about a friend or relative helping you with childcare, that you already know who that person is. While this can be a rich and rewarding childcare arrangement for all concerned, it does need thought and preparation to ensure it works smoothly. Whether this is the only childcare you use – or an additional childcare arrangement to others – you don't want to ruin your relationships with your nearest and dearest.

As with all kinds of childcare, you are not going to be happy with the arrangement if you feel your child's and your own needs are not being met. You need to take the time upfront to work out what you want. It cannot be stressed enough how important it is to discuss things before you start – this will avoid many issues – and as we all know it is so much harder to undo something once it is done.

Try filling in the grid below. This will help you to finalise your criteria and also help you think about any worries or concerns you have about the arrangement. An example is given to show you how to enter your information.

When	*Three afternoons a week: Monday, Tuesday and Thursday.*
For whom	*Both children: 18 months and 3 years.*
Where	*At home and occasionally at Mum's.*
Will need to	*Collect from childminder.* *Give them tea.* *Occasionally bath them if I am running late.*
Worries or concerns	*Mum getting tired.* *Mum not keeping a close enough eye on safety.* *Children getting away with too much, particularly little boy.* *Children not being made to eat enough of the right food.* *Coming to happy agreement about finances and time.*

When	
For whom	
Where	
Will need to	
Worries or concerns	

'You get such joy watching them grow up. You have more time to spend with them than you had as a mum, and you really appreciate it.' – Sarah, grandmother

Discussing your needs

Do discuss your needs, concerns and worries rather than just leaving your child with a slightly bewildered aunt and heading for the hills. Take time to think about the relationship with your friend or relative, where you think any problems could arise and what you think is the best way of laying down the ground rules. Your friend or relative may feel that this is totally unnecessary and that you are being too pedantic. You may need to stress that it is easier this way and it will make you feel more relaxed, as you know that things will be working for you as well as for him or her. It is also a good opportunity for your friend or relative to air any worries or concerns.

> *'They think they are young and energetic enough but can they really do it? If I am on my knees, what will they be feeling like?'*

The first thing you need to do is ensure that your friend or relative is genuinely pleased to, and wants to, help. Otherwise things can start to go wrong from the beginning. You also need to look at yourself and whether you are going to be able to manage the relationship well.

Things will work better if you already have a good, open relationship. You both need to have the ability to be honest with each other and take onboard and act on what the other says. It obviously makes things a lot easier if you have similar values and principles about bringing up children.

> *'I do find them tiring if I try to live my normal life at the same time. It is easier when you just concentrate on them. The advantage of being a grandmother is that you can give them more time and I think it really helps to build their confidence.' – Elizabeth, grandmother*

If one of your parents is going to help, he or she may like to contact the Grandparents' Association (see Useful Sources of Information, page 217). This has an advice line and produces fact sheets and publications that deal with some of the potential ups and downs he or she may encounter. They also run grandparent and toddler groups; there may be one in your area.

> *'I find it invigorating, rather than tiring.' – Sarah, grandmother*

Questions to ask

Commitment and resources

- Are you truly keen and happy to do this?
- How many hours a week would you be happy to do? Which days suit you best?
- I am worried about how exhausted you will be. Do you really think you are fit enough? What other commitments do you have in the week?
- Shall we give it a trial period for a month and see how everyone feels?
- Are you happy to pick up from pre-school every day?
- Would you be able to keep the children until 7pm one day a week so I can work late?

> *'They can really start to resent it — they can't accept invitations from their friends, yet it is not a job. You are stopping them from leading their life.'*

Beliefs and principles

- I feel strongly about x, y and z when it comes to bringing up children. How do you feel about these areas?
- What areas do you feel particularly strongly about and why?
- It is very important for the children that we are consistent with our discipline. Are you happy to do this? (Talk through how you would like your children to be disciplined, giving examples.)
- If you have a different idea for disciplining that you think might work, will you discuss it with me first?
- What are your views on treats, TV, table manners, blankets or comfort toys and dummies? (Discuss anything else where you think opinions may differ.)
- How do you think we should solve an issue on which we don't agree?

> *'I find it very difficult when my daughter tells me to discipline my granddaughter. I feel really mean, and have to tell her that I am doing it because mummy says so.'* — Sarah, grandmother

Safety and hygiene

- Would you be happy for me to send you on a first aid course – for your peace of mind, and mine?
- Are you happy for me to come round and toddler-proof your house – for the safety of the children and your possessions!
- I fret about the children picking up infections. Are you happy to keep your kitchen and bathroom super-clean? Will you remember to get the children to wash their hands before lunch?

Food, rest and routine

- It is really important for me, and the children, that they follow their normal routine. Are you happy to ensure this happens?
- Are you happy to cook for them each evening? Shall I create a simple menu sheet with some ideas or shall I prepare some food and put it in your freezer?
- Are you happy to stick to my rules on table manners?
- The baby needs to start solids in a month. Are you happy to help with this?
- My daughter needs to have a rest at lunchtime for about two hours – can you ensure you are at home then? Can I set a cot up in your spare room?
- Are you happy to use my method for settling her down for her sleep? If you think of a better way of getting her to sleep will you please discuss it with me first?

> *'My daughter-in-law does not set too rigid boundaries and leaves it up to my judgment. I think it makes it easier for me as she respects my way of dealing with the children.' – Celia, grandmother*

Activities and development

- Would you be happy to take them to the local toddler group?
- Are you happy if they have a friend to play, or would you find it too much?
- They really need a good dose of fresh air and activity every day. Can you cater for this?
- Are you happy to take them on outings now and again? I will obviously give you the necessary money.
- Here is a list of activities they like. Are you happy with these? What other activities do you think you would enjoy doing with them? What equipment or toys can I bring over to help you?
- Will you ensure, if they are watching TV, they only watch the DVDs I have brought you?
- Are you happy to help with potty training?

> *'We are a different generation, teaching them different things and from a different perspective. A 20-year-old can't do that for them.' – Tim, grandfather*

Holidays and illness

- How should we arrange our holidays to suit each other?
- Is there someone who can help if you are ill or have an appointment? Why don't I see who I can find that I would be happy with?
- Can you give me plenty of warning if you think you will be unable to help on a certain day?

To pay or not to pay

This can be a difficult area, and again it is better to be up front. You want something that suits everyone otherwise resentment will build up, on one side or both. Unless you really can't afford to pay, do try to give some sort of recompense. For example, you could say, 'As well as paying for the children's food and other expenses, I would like to pay you an hourly rate, I was thinking about …, what were you thinking about?'

> *'Do try to pay if you can. It clarifies the relationship; it is like putting on a suit and going to work. They are now working and being paid in recognition of the job they are doing.'*

If not paying, always try to give some benefit in kind. There are many things you could do for free that would be appreciated. Discuss ideas such as a contribution towards a holiday or a car, some help with DIY, gardening or building work.

Whether you are paying or not, your friend or relative will always try that little bit harder for you, so do give gifts now and again to show your appreciation. As long as they are thoughtful, they need not be expensive.

> *'It is very easy not to recognise a family member. Payment is a form of recognition and would have made it work better for us. Even though my husband was setting up a business, money was tight and my mum was insistent we didn't pay, I think it would have been better.'*

Formalities

For everyone's peace of mind, you may want to treat the arrangement like any other childcare job – checking references, having a Criminal Records Bureau check done and arranging suitable insurance. See Chapter 12 (page 177) for further details.

Tips for your parenting style

Following on from the questionnaire in Chapter 1 (see page 23), here are some tips and ideas for working with a friend or a relative. You should take note of the points for your stronger style(s), or you may like to read through all of them!

> *'Because it is casual and not set up with holidays, if something comes up, like cousin Mark coming from Oregon, they then can't help. I felt I never had the confidence that she would definitely be able to help the next week. With no guaranteed childcare, I couldn't plan the week. I found it hugely annoying.'*

Keep them safe

- Let them know if you are worried about safety or another issue – don't assume that they are already aware of your concerns. They can then work to put your mind at rest.
- Be aware of being too involved. Tell and show them what to do, then let them get on with it; you can't build your trust in someone if you don't let them do the job.
- Don't let too many of your emotions show when you are stressed – it will only have a negative effect on everyone. Always try to remain as calm as possible.
- If you are worried that their house is not as clean as yours, or that they are not keeping your house as clean as you would like, try to be diplomatic about how you broach the subject.

Freedom

- It is very important that you and your friend or relative agree on the routine and structure of the day.
- Ensure at hand-over times you give them enough information, including contact numbers, and do not race out of the door thinking they will manage fine because they know you well.
- Don't let them become complacent just because you are fairly easy going. Ensure you deal with issues, rather than letting things go.
- Give plenty of warning if you are going to be late for some reason. Try not to let it become a habit. If it does become a habit, recognise this and think how you can either make amends or rearrange the hours.

Traditional

- Ensure they are happy to work to your set routine.
- Make sure they are happy to discipline and reward as you prefer, and if your child is old enough, to work at making your child do the right thing the next time around.
- Ensure you are not too direct or abrupt with them if you feel things are not running as they should. They will be trying hard and it may take a bit of time to get into the swing of it.
- If they really prefer to do something in a different way, do consider it – children can be very good at doing things one way at one person's house and another way at home.

CHAPTER 10

Nannies, Maternity Nurses and Night Nannies

This chapter will take you through each step of finding and working well with a nanny, maternity or night nanny. There are additional details on each of these, including pros and cons, in Chapter 3 (see page 45). This chapter will help you to sort out the live-in or live-out dilemma, search, screen and interview and make the final decision.

Nannies

What you can expect from them

They will attend to all your child's needs while in their care. These are often referred to as nursery duties:

- Planning and preparing children's meals and baby's feeds.
- Dressing and washing of children.
- Caring for and playing with the children.
- Washing and ironing their clothes.
- Keeping child-related areas clean: kitchen, playrooms, bedrooms and bathrooms.

Importantly, nannies take full responsibility for your children, working hard to ensure their safety at all times. They should also help your children to develop key skills and abilities in line with their developmental milestones.

> *'You become a lot closer to the children than you would when working in a nursery.' – Clare, nanny to three children*

Hours

A full-time nanny generally works five days a week with weekends off, but this can be open to negotiation. While hours are totally negotiable, live-in nannies tend to work approximately 11 hours a day and live-out nannies up to 10 hours a day.

Costs

Live-out nannies are usually paid more than live-in as they do not have the benefit of board and lodging. They are generally paid between £300 and £500 per week (net, i.e. excluding tax) with extra for babysitting. Live-in nannies are generally paid between £230 and £350 per week (net), often including one or two nights' babysitting. If your nanny applies for registration with the Voluntary Childcare Register you may be eligible for Tax Credits from the Government or Childcare Vouchers from your employer (see page 177 for details).

Qualifications

There are a number of childcare qualifications a nanny could have:

- CACHE Diploma in Childcare and Education (previously known as NNEB).
- NVQ or SVQ Level 3 in Children's Care, Learning and Development.
- BTEC National Award, Certificate or Diploma in Children's Care, Learning and Development.
- BTEC Higher National Certificate or Diploma in Advanced Practice in Work with Children and Families.
- A first-aid training qualification.

(See page 207 for a more detailed explanation of each of these qualifications.)

However, you do not need any qualifications to work as a nanny, so some nannies will be equipped solely with well-earned experience.

Please note: As there is no national register of nannies, it is very important to check references. You can also obtain a Criminal Records Bureau check to put your mind further at rest.

Special needs

Nannies and maternity nurses can be a fantastic childcare resource if you have a child with special needs. They can give them the individual care and attention they require as well as taking them to any appointments they may have.

> *'I really encourage my nannies or au pairs to get involved with my child's treatments. They then know what needs to be achieved and feel part of it, and often come up with good ideas.'*

Some nannies and maternity nurses specialise in children with special needs and may have had additional training. Alternatively, you may like to employ someone who has no special training but is keen to learn and gain experience.

> *'In-home childcare must be confident and outgoing. They must be happy to take your child out and about and deal with all the ups and downs which that can bring.'*

Nanny share

Nowadays nannies come in a variety of forms to suit different people and different lifestyles. Nanny shares are growing in popularity as they can greatly increase your options in terms of part-time childcare, lower costs and greater flexibility.

You can enter into an agreed nanny share with another family where your children are either:

- Looked after together in one of your homes.
- Looked after separately at different times, for example, two days with one family and three days with the other or mornings with one family and afternoons with another.

Nannies who work for three or more families may have to register as a childminder.

Nanny share pros	✓	Nanny share cons	✗
Makes what can be unaffordable affordable, particularly if you have one child.		Families may not have the same ideas about rules, discipline and feeding.	
Administration is shared – tax, National Insurance, etc.		Coordinating holidays and days off can be difficult.	
If you work from home, your children could be looked after in the other home, leaving you in peace.		Wear and tear can be an issue if the children are looked after in only one house.	
Your children can have other children to socialise with.		Not only do you have to manage the relationship with the nanny, but also with the other family.	
If the nanny is unable to make it to work, there are more people to work on arranging emergency cover.		One family may be happier with the nanny than the other, or the nanny may be happier with one family than the other.	
If there are problems with the nanny there is another party to discuss and address the problems with.		If one family pulls out of the arrangement, the other family may be left in the lurch.	

'You end up competing for time, so you must set everything in stone. Personally, I think it is easier if you don't do it with a friend.'

Part-time nanny

A part-time nanny can be employed either by the day, by the half day or by the hour. You may have set hours each week or it may be on a more ad hoc basis. The nanny may have other nanny work or a different job altogether.

Part-time nanny pros	✓	Part-time nanny cons	✗
Makes what can be unaffordable affordable, particularly if you have one child.		It can take longer for you and your children to build up a relationship with your nanny.	
The nanny may be self-employed, in which case you do not need to worry about tax and National Insurance.		Handovers can take longer as there can be more for you to tell a nanny who does not see the children as often.	
Generally, part-time nannies are live-out so there is less infringement of your privacy.		You can end up doing a lot of the organisation for the days the nanny works as she is not there the day before to prepare things	

Male nannies (or mannies)

Some high-profile celebrity hirings and various press articles and books have helped to bring the 'manny' to the fore. The world-renowned Norland College now takes male students and a male nanny is indeed an increasingly popular option. However, despite its notoriety, the percentage of mannies in the UK is still extremely low.

Manny pros	✓	Manny cons	✗
Great if you have children who need to burn off lots of energy.		Your partner may be less keen on the idea than you.	
Can be a good male role model for your children.		Your food bill may increase more than with a female nanny.	
Some are reputed to be better at ironing than their female counterparts!		Some are reported to be less domestically adept.	
They can be more practical and hands on around the house – mending a drawer in the children's bedroom, etc.		Some of your friends may feel uncomfortable about it, particularly if their children are girls.	

Nanny-housekeeper

Once seen as austere women running large homes, housekeepers are now being employed much more frequently, and in smaller homes. Quite a few agencies specialise in bringing people from abroad, for example from the Philippines.

> 'First time around I did the classic of hiring someone who only did kids' stuff. Now I have someone who does things like service the car and do the dry cleaning; she often seems to enjoy doing those things more and I think she likes the variety.'

Duties

While housekeepers traditionally only attend to the running of the house, more and more are also looking after children. These nanny-housekeepers are prepared to take over most household duties as well as assisting with childcare.

> 'She gets them to do things with her, like hanging up the laundry, and they are all having fun. I respect her for that and also feel relief that I don't have to do those jobs.'

Hours

Nanny-housekeepers will usually work five days a week. While hours are totally negotiable, a live-in nanny-housekeeper tends to work approximately 11 hours a day and a live-out one up to 10 hours a day.

> 'She works from 8.30am to 6pm, but if it is a quiet afternoon I am happy for her to go out and do some things for herself. If she works extra hours I also ensure I pay her. She waves me away but I stick to it.'

Costs

An experienced nanny-housekeeper will be paid towards the higher end of the nanny scale, at around £400–500 live out and £300–350 live in (net, i.e. after tax).

> 'It is a luxury but when I put together the cost of the cleaner we used to have, the babysitting and the nanny we had one day a week it is not that much more. She makes us both far more relaxed, makes our life better and I am a better mother.'

Nanny-housekeeper pros	✓	Nanny-housekeeper cons	✗
They will take on all household duties.		They can be an expensive option.	
They offer great flexibility as they can do whatever needs to be done – including those things you don't want to do!		It can sometimes be hard to find a housekeeper who is happy to do the percentage split of household duties and childcare that you prefer.	
They can negate the need for any additional help in the form of cleaning, ironing, etc.		They have access to even more of your home life than a nanny, so you lose even more privacy.	
They tend to stay for longer periods of time than a nanny.		Employers must try not to take advantage of the fact that they can do everything – they will probably not be able to run the house to perfection and look after the children full time. Realistic expectations are needed.	
They really can make life easier! A very good option if you have one child, school-aged children or do not need someone to have sole charge the entire time.		The majority of housekeepers will be looking for a live-in position.	

'I have struggled to find that 60:40 housekeeper split of 60 per cent around the home and 40 per cent with the children.'

Maternity nurse

Maternity nurses usually provide 24-hour live-in care for the first few weeks of your baby's life. They can take sole charge of a newborn, but normally work alongside the mother.

Hours

They are on call 24 hours a day, six days a week (although you should allow them to get some rest!). They should get one full day off each week.

Costs

As a result of their hours, they are expensive and can cost anything from £600 (gross, i.e. before tax) a week upwards. You may well have to pay more for multiple births. They are self-employed and so will deal with their own tax and National Insurance.

Qualifications

The majority of maternity nurses are simply nannies who are very experienced, particularly with newborn babies. Some may be qualified nurses or midwives. There are some three-day or week-long intensive maternity nurse courses, which experienced nannies or midwives use to top up their skills. The best qualifications will be accredited by a recognised awarding body, such as CACHE.

Night nanny

Night nannies are usually qualified nannies who stay overnight and take sole charge and then leave in the morning. They carry out all childcare duties, such as night feeds, settling the child to sleep, changing nappies and getting the child up and dressed in the morning.

Hours

A standard night booking is usually from 8pm or 9pm until 7am, however you can, of course, agree different hours to suit you.

Costs

You can expect to pay something in the region of £8 per hour and if using an agency anything from £10 to £25 per night to the agency as well. For longer-term bookings, the agency fee may drop after an initial period. The agency may also ask for an introduction fee.

> 'We employed a night nanny for a week when my son was 7 weeks old. I was a bit reluctant to do it but was also absolutely exhausted. However, she was great, she got my son into a better routine and I felt like a new person after a week of more normal sleep.'

Live-in or live-out?

For some people looking for a nanny, the live-in or live-out debate is a non-starter. You may all be squeezed into your home as it is, with simply no room for one extra. Alternatively, you may have a separate flat that is screaming 'Nanny, please live here'. For those in the middle, it can be a tricky decision as there are pros and cons on both sides.

> *'My husband was totally against live-in help. I persuaded him to try it for two months – we have now had live-in nannies or au pairs for four years!'*

Use the table below to help you move towards a decision. Mark a tick or cross next to any points that particularly resonate with you:

Live-in pros	✓	Live-in cons	✗
Cheaper than a live-out nanny.		Your household bills will increase.	
More flexibility in terms of when they work, e.g. they could start very early or work very late.		You lose a lot of your privacy.	
They are less likely to be late for work.		You may feel awkward about whether to share mealtimes and how to broach this.	
Babysitting is likely to be more easily arranged at short notice.		You will need to provide them with suitable accommodation: their own room, a TV, preferably a double bed, internet and phone.	
If there is an emergency in the night or you go into labour, they will be able to stay and look after the other children.		You may not like some of their personal habits – and they may not like some of yours!	

> *'You have such trepidation about someone living in your home, about how it will affect the family, but such desperation because you need the help.'*

Live-out pros	✓	Live-out cons	✗
When they leave at the end of the day, your house is your own and you all have a break from each other.		A more expensive option.	
You may find it easier to keep the relationship on a more professional footing than with a live-in nanny.		They can be late for work and this will then impact on your day.	
You can be less involved in their personal life and what they do out of work.		They may have more sick days off than a live-in nanny.	
They won't do annoying things such as using up all the hot water.		You may have to negotiate harder if you need them to stay late for some reason or want them to stay overnight.	

Searching

After much contemplation, you have decided what you want. Well done, first major decision made! Now, follow the next few steps to work out exactly what you need from that person.

Writing a job description

One of the first things you should do is draw up a basic job description, which can be used as a job advert, to brief an agency or when putting the word out with friends. It will help to avoid an influx of irrelevant applications and will help you to sift through and weed out the wrong candidates and find the right ones.

A job description can be as long or short as you like, whatever you feel suits you and the job you would like done. You can always expand on it before your new employee arrives but it is good to write the basics down now. It will help you in your search and you can send it to prospective candidates so they know exactly what the job entails. Your final choice can agree to it before she starts. See page 210 for an example.

> 'You must be so clear up front about what you want. I thought it would be obvious and subsequently we hired the wrong person. I simply didn't give it enough thought.'

If employing a maternity nurse or night nanny for the first time, you may want to take more direction from her in terms of what she can do for you. However, be clear up front about what you want out of the arrangement. If you get a maternity nurse or night nanny that really suits your family you may want to ask the same one back again, as each new child arrives.

> *'While my maternity nurse let me know I was ultimately in charge, I was not entirely sure what I was doing! She gently guided me and gave me choices about what I would like her to do.'*

Who will suit your family?

Having worked out what you want your new childcarer to do for you, you need to think further about the characteristics and attributes you would like her to have. Think about both 'Must have' and 'Would be nice' characteristics and skills. The table below gives examples of characteristics and skills you may be looking for.

Must have	Would be nice
Have recognised childcare qualification.	Have helped look after three children including a baby.
Have had sole charge of at least two children under the age of four.	Have driven children in a previous job.
Be happy to have shared charge on Thursdays and Fridays.	Have stayed in a job for at least two years.
Be a driver and non-smoker.	Be tidy and organised.
Be able to plan and cook good healthy meals.	Have friends around here or know other nannies in the area.
Have a can-do attitude and sense of humour.	Enjoy swimming.

See page 209 for a further list of characteristics that you may want to look for.

> *'It is good that we respect each other and we stand by each other in front of the kids. It is great when a nanny has good manners and teaches good manners.'*

Putting it all together

You should now be in a position to answer all of the headings below. This will form the basis of your search. The first table gives an example of how you might fill in the information.

What	Nanny share.
When	Two days a week.
For whom	A 2-year-old girl and new baby due.
Where	Small village outside Bristol.
Family and lifestyle	Friendly and outdoors-orientated family.
Main duties	Shared charge.
Skills needed	Recognised qualification, driver, first-aid trained.
Characteristics	Cheerful, caring, reliable, lots of initiative.
Contact	Laura 01234 56789 after 6pm.

What	
When	
For whom	
Where	
Family and lifestyle	
Main duties	
Skills needed	
Characteristics	
Contact	

The main search options

Different people have different ways of doing things. Some would rather use an agency, others would rather save money and remain more in control by using a website or magazine ad. Others prefer only to find people via word of mouth.

Agencies

There are now hundreds of nanny, maternity-nurse and home-help agencies offering to find the right person for you. Some pros and cons of agencies are detailed below, followed by ideas on finding a good one and getting the best out of them.

Agency pros	✓	Agency cons	✗
They do the work for you – a real benefit if you are short of time.		The most expensive option – usually the equivalent of one month's nanny wages.	
They are experienced in the area and can help you to assess your needs.		With no industry standards or regulations, it can be quite daunting choosing an agency.	
They do the initial screening and background checking, so you only see the best-suited candidates.		Can offer only a limited number of candidates.	
It is easier to negotiate wages and terms of the job through a third party.		They could be sourcing candidates from the same websites you are looking at – but charging a large fee.	
They offer support, help and advice not only through the hiring but for an initial period after the beginning of the job.		You can feel less in control of the process.	
If the first nanny does not work out within a certain period they offer a guaranteed replacement.		You can find yourself doing some/most of the work and then paying for the privilege.	
You only pay them when they have found someone for you.		Some can oversell your position resulting in a disappointed and aggrieved nanny.	
Competition is fierce and less agencies are requesting an introduction or joining fee.		Some may not have a very rigorous screening and checking process.	

Dealing with agencies successfully

A word-of-mouth recommendation is always worth paying attention to, but should always be followed up by your own checks. While there are few industry standards it is a good sign if the agency is a member of the Recruitment and Employment Federation (REC) or the Association of Nanny Agencies (ANA).

> *'They helped me work out what I wanted and then sent me three CVs that were all brilliant.'*

Questions to ask

- What are your charges and when are they payable?
- What is your replacement/guarantee policy? (This should be at least 6 weeks.)
- Where do you recruit your nannies? (Nannies will approach those agencies with a good reputation. Agencies should not just search the internet where you could find them yourself.)
- Do you interview all your nannies in person? (At the same time they should check originals of documentation to confirm their identity and qualifications.)
- What background/reference checks do you perform? Are you happy for me to carry out my own reference check?
- What support service do you provide after the placement is made?
- How long have you been in business? (Usually the longer the better.)
- Would you mind if I asked two of your previous clients for a reference about your agency?

> *'One agency pressured me into going for interviews for jobs I did not want. They didn't listen to what I wanted out of a job and I presume they did not listen to what parents wanted from a nanny. I found a much better agency that helped me find a job that was right for me.'*
> *— Bethan, nanny to two children*

What you need to do

- When choosing an agency ensure they sound competent over the phone. If they are not prompt in returning your phone calls, look elsewhere.
- Trust you instincts. If you don't think they are right for you, look elsewhere.
- Give as detailed and realistic a picture as possible of the job and your family. Be honest about particularly difficult children and so on.
- You must make the final decision on who to interview and you must interview candidates yourself.

- If you are not happy with the CVs you are sent and/or the candidates you interview, be as detailed as possible about why you didn't like what they sent you and what you would like to see instead. You have to help them to help you.
- Let them know as soon as possible if your circumstances change or there is a change in your brief.
- Check references yourself (by phone) even if the agency says it has done so.

Websites

These can be a fantastic source for finding someone, but there is a bit of time and effort involved.

General community

These websites have ads for almost anything you can imagine from flat shares to cars for sale. They list jobs as well as details of people looking for jobs. The most well known in the UK is gumtree.com. Depending on the site it may be free to display your ad or you may have to pay a fee of approximately £20.

> *'For me, flexibility is the number one thing I need, but you must explain what you mean by flexible.'*

Specialised community

These are like the community websites but they specialise in childcare. They will have families offering jobs and childcarers offering their services. They may be attached to a parenting or childcare information or discussion website. A family is usually charged between £10 and £30 to post an ad. Examples include: nannyjob.co.uk, greatcare.co.uk and nannyselect.co.uk.

> *'You must be straightforward and honest about the job. No one benefits if you aren't.'*

Nanny-share sites

These put you in contact with possible nannies and with other families in your area, who are also looking for a nanny share. The fee is usually around £20 to £25. Examples include: thenannysharers.co.uk and nannyshare.co.uk.

Website pros	✓	Website cons	✗
Your job posting goes global!		The candidates are usually not screened – anyone can offer their services.	
A much cheaper option – most sites charge between £10 and £40, and some are free.		The onus is very much on you and how thorough you are prepared to be with interviewing and reference checking.	
There are usually many potential candidates to choose from as it is usually free for them to post their details.		If employing an overseas nanny you may not meet her until she arrives in your home. If it does not work out, you will need to sort out suitable arrangements for the nanny.	
You can do it all from the comfort of your own home and at any time of day or night. You are very much in control of the search.		You may have to help an overseas nanny with her visa and entry requirements.	
Not only do you look at their details but they can look at yours and choose you.		There are scams on both sides – bogus nannies and bogus families – never send money to a stranger.	
You can find someone very quickly.		You may need to re-post your details to keep the ad current.	
Sites often store your details, so if you need a new nanny you can simply update your details.		The market is crowded. There is little loyalty. People are snapped up quickly so the search can be long and frustrating.	

Posting your website ad

Before you post an ad, look through other ads to get an idea of what people are saying and what you think works well. There are so many jobs advertised that you need to try to make yours stand out and be appealing without sounding too whacky or desperate. If you can, include a photo of you and your children. See page 211 for an example of an ad for a nanny.

> *'I so wish I could afford to find a nanny through an agency, but I have found two great au pairs through websites and my current nanny through a magazine ad. It just takes some effort.'*

Magazines

Placing ads in magazines has dipped in popularity as the internet is such a popular medium. However, most of the relevant magazines now have jobs listed in the magazine and on job boards on their website. This is often a good way of finding a more experienced nanny. Also, if you want a nanny with certain skills, for example, a nanny/groom, you can advertise in a magazine dedicated to that area. See page 211 for an example of an ad for a nanny and page 220 for details of magazines in which you might advertise.

Magazines pros	✓	Magazines cons	✗
They are relatively cheap.		They can have a very limited time frame.	
They reach a very specific and targeted audience.		You only have a very small space in which to sell your job.	
They can be useful for finding help with particular skills.		A misprint cannot be corrected so you must ensure all details are absolutely right.	
Most national magazines now have online job listings.		Paper-based magazines are not as popular with younger job seekers.	
You can now submit your ad online or by email to most magazines.		Distribution and readership levels can be quite small.	
Local magazines can find you local people who prefer to live out.		A lot of those looking in the national magazines may be looking for live-in positions.	

Other places for ads

You can also place ads:

- In local shops.
- On community notice boards.
- At childcare training colleges.

The pros and cons are similar to those associated with magazine ads.

'You want to know what the family is like – are they more laissez faire or are they quite strict and Victorian?' – Clare, nanny to three children

Word of mouth

Some people are only happy if they find someone via word of mouth; others see it as a way to ruin a friendship. Quite a few people prefer to find their maternity nurses in this way. If using this method to find childcare, make sure you are very specific about what you want. You may like to send out an email so that people can then forward it to their friends.

Word of mouth pros	✓	Word of mouth cons	✗
Cheap!		Can be awkward if you employ someone and it does not work out.	
From a trusted source who knows you and/or the candidate.		You will be looking in a limited pool and are not guaranteed a result.	
The candidate will probably be tried and tested.		Different people have different ideas of what good childcare is.	
Can be quite a speedy search option if the right person is available and not far away.		Different people can run their homes in very different ways.	
You may be able to find out more about the candidate than with a traditional referee.		Someone may gloss over the bad bits in giving a reference in order to move their nanny on easily.	

'Don't get desperate and employ anyone because you are so grateful that they want to come and work for you. Take your time – it will be worth it in the end.'

Someone from abroad

If you are thinking about employing someone from abroad, either from an English-speaking country, such as Australia or Canada, or from somewhere else such as Eastern Europe or the Philippines, see Chapter 11 (see page 165).

'Because she is working to send money back home, she works really hard – she has more to gain and more to lose. The downside is that I lose her for a month every year when she flies home.'

Screening

Creating an assessment sheet

You may feel this is slightly over the top, but it will make your screening and final decision-making a lot easier. You could use the assessment sheet on page 212 (you can make copies of this sheet so that you have one for each candidate) or alter this sheet so that it suits you better. (See page 143 and page 209 for examples of 'must have' and 'would be nice' characteristics and skills.) It can be helpful to put stars next to points you think are particularly important, or question marks next to things that worry you. Make sure you check any relevant documentation, such as proof of identity and childcare qualifications.

Use your initial screening to get three or four candidates for either a telephone or face-to-face interview.

Making a shortlist

Go through your prospective candidates and screen them into groups of Yes, No and Maybe. Be strict with your screening as you do not want to waste their time or yours.

- **Yes:** Communicate with them further so that you can find out a bit more about each other. It is important that you both have all the necessary information before deciding to go forward to a more in-depth interview.

> **Important note:** Always give a realistic and measured overview of the job and your family. Do not oversell the job as someone will arrive, be disappointed, become unmotivated and probably leave.

- **No:** Tell them no, sooner rather than later. Always take the time to thank people for their application and to let them know you will not be taking things further.
- **Maybe:** If you can, keep those who nearly fit the bill on hold.

'When they want a job, you have the power; as soon as they are in the job, that all changes. You need to know what you want when you have the power, before they start.'

Interviewing

While people find being interviewed quite nerve racking, they don't often pause to think that the interviewer might be more nervous than them! Preparing well will help you to feel calmer. Remember, a candidate will always look to you to take control.

If you are interviewing people from abroad you may only be able to interview them by phone. (See page 167 for tips on interviewing by phone.)

Interviewing face to face

- Ask candidates to bring all their relevant documentation with them to an interview. Try to interview in your home so they can meet the children and see where they will work.
- Offer something to drink and make them feel welcome. This will relax both of you.
- If possible, introduce the candidate to the children at the beginning of the interview. Make sure they are as clean, tidy and well behaved as possible!
- In most cases you should offer to pay travel expenses; ensure you have the necessary money.
- If possible, get your partner to meet your preferred candidates.

Interview structure and questions

Plan this in advance. Make notes as you go through the interview – you may like to use a scoring system, for example:

3 = ideal/above requirements

2 = adequate

1 = below requirements/needs development

You can then transfer any key points and the scores onto your assessment sheets.

> *'If the person interviewing you is relaxed, it makes you more relaxed.' – Clare, nanny to three children*

Here are some suggestions for structuring an interview:

The job

Concisely explain the nature of the job; you may like to include details of:

- How much or how little you and/or your partner will be around.
- Further information, such as use of car, their accommodation, petty cash and any house rules you feel they might take exception to.
- Benefits to them, such as other nannies in the area, perks of the job and the area.
- How you like to work with your childcarer.

Remember you *must* be honest and not give unrealistic expectations of the job.

> *'Tell the truth in the job interview — you have to manage their expectations.'*

All about them

Review their CV and experience. Always ensure you have a copy of anything they have sent you. Don't just say 'Tell me about yourself'.

- Ask relevant questions about the areas that interest you, or any gaps you are worried about.
- Find out what elements they particularly liked or disliked about previous work and/or education.
- Ask about reasons for leaving jobs or doing particular courses.
- Ask them if there is anything else they would like to add.

Additional questions

It is important to have a list of prepared questions. Try to ask questions around the qualities you are interested in. To give you a few ideas, here are some of the more common questions that people ask.

> *'It is nice when you can meet the children first. The parents can then see how you relate to them straight away.'* — Bethan, nanny to two children

General nanny questions

- What do you like about working with children?
- What is it about being a nanny, in particular, that appeals to you?
- What characteristics do you have that you think help you work well with children?
- Have you been involved in an emergency situation with a child? If so, what happened and how did you deal with it?

- If a child was choking on a small object what would you do? (Or burned his or her arm or fell off a wall?)
- What sorts of activities would you recommend for the age my children are at?
- Do you enjoy cooking? What sort of meals would you prepare for my children?
- Have you got any medical history I should be aware of?
- Why are you particularly interested in this job?
- What characteristics do you like in an employer?
- What are your long-term goals?
- Would I be able to contact your referees by phone? What times would be most convenient?

> *'With both of my nannies at the beginning there was a lot of creativity and art, but it dwindled over time.'*

More in-depth nanny/nanny-share questions

- Have you dealt with difficult eaters? Have you found any methods that work?
- Have you potty trained any children?
- What are your views on rests and sleep?
- What are your views on TV and DVD watching?
- Have you ever disagreed with a parent on an aspect of childcare? If so, how did you deal with it? If not, how would you deal with it?
- Do you have any recommendations for keeping the children's environment safe?
- How do you think children should be disciplined?
- What is your view on tantrums and how to deal with them?
- Have you dealt with a particularly difficult child? If so, tell me about it and what you think you did that made a difference.
- Do you see any difficulties arising out of a nanny-share/part-time nanny arrangement?
- Have you been part of a nanny share before? If so, what worked and what did not?
- I can receive Childcare Vouchers from my employer. Are you familiar with these and are you registered on the Voluntary Childcare Register? If you are not, would you be interested in becoming registered?

> *'We decided to try it out and if it didn't work it didn't work. It was the best thing we could have done. It worked well.'*

Nanny-housekeeper questions

- What do you think is the secret of a well-run household?
- What balance of childcare to housekeeping do you prefer?
- What tasks do you prefer doing? Is there anything you would rather not do?
- How do you prefer to work with your employer in terms of running the house? And in terms of childcare?

Maternity nurse/night nanny questions

- What sort of routine do you like to encourage?
- What are your views on breast- and bottle-feeding?
- What are the most common newborn problems you find yourself dealing with? How do you deal with/what are your views on these?
- Tell me about your first-aid qualifications.
- What sort of emergencies have you dealt with in the past? What did you do?
- What sort of routine do you like for yourself when working?
- How do you like to work with the mother? How do you like to interact with the family?
- Are you happy to help with my older children at times/in a crisis?
- Do you smoke?

Pay and benefits

When you feel you have gathered enough information, talk about pay and additional benefits. If the candidate has interviewed well, make sure they are clear on pay, hours, time off, holiday entitlement, car use, amount of sole charge, live-in details and so on.

Holiday entitlement

The statutory minimum for paid holiday is 28 days a year including Bank Holidays (from 1 October 2008).

Wrapping up

Don't give an answer at the end of the interview. You need time to think about everything you have heard and also to think of anything you may have missed out. Thank them for their time and say when you will contact them. Don't be afraid to say you are interviewing other people.

Making up your mind

Always keep track of who you have seen and what you thought of them. You may find that you have an outright winner. If not, the fact that you have taken a systematic approach should pay off. Look at the sheets from the interviews. Who has the most positive points? Who did you feel right about? It is important that you use both your head and heart, not just one or the other.

Second interview or short-term trial

You may like to ask your shortlist – or just your favoured candidate – back for a second time. If possible, this interview should be longer and more relaxed; it could be for two hours, half a day or a full day. She should spend time with your children and see how your household works. It will help you make up your mind or confirm you have made the right decision. If relevant, come to a suitable financial arrangement. If your partner has not already done so, get him to meet her or interview her on the phone.

Offering the job

Hopefully, when you offer the job, your chosen candidate will say yes! However, do be prepared for her to say she has decided that it is not the right job for her. It is probably not a good idea to try to persuade her otherwise. You want someone who is keen, not someone you have had to beg.

> **Quick tip:** If your prospective childcarer wants more money than you are offering and you feel you cannot stretch that far, you could offer additional time off, a pay review after three or six months or some other benefit.

Once someone has accepted your job offer, you need to breathe a sigh of relief and then check references (see page 179) and carry out a Criminal Records Bureau check (see page 180).

> *'She is great at the little things – the pyjamas all laid out and toothpaste on brushes for bath time.'*

Tips for your parenting style

Following on from the questionnaire in Chapter 1 (see page 23), here are some tips and ideas for working with in-home childcare, such as nannies, for each of the styles. You should take note of the points for your stronger style(s), or you may like to read through all of them!

Keep them safe

- Let her know if you are worried about safety or another issue, discuss what she could do to put your mind at rest and also ask for her suggestions and ideas.
- Be aware of being too involved in your nanny's or maternity nurse's job. Tell and show her what to do but then let her get on with the job, particularly if she is experienced and well qualified. Not giving her enough trust and responsibility will de-motivate her.
- Don't let too many of your emotions show when you are stressed. Always try to remain as calm as possible in front of your employee.
- Ensure that you and your childcarer are consistent in how you discipline and treat your children.

 'I am given lots of responsibility and so I feel more trusted, reliable and capable. You can feel that you are learning as you go. If a parent breathes down your neck it is harder to learn.' – Clare, nanny to three children

Freedom

- Ensure your nanny or maternity nurse knows you don't like things too structured. It is very important that you are both in agreement about routines.
- Find a nanny who is fun and creative.
- Ensure at handover times you give enough information, including contact numbers and any possible problems. Do not race out of the door leaving her in at the deep end – it will make things harder for her and your children.
- As you are fairly easy-going, don't let your nanny or maternity nurse become complacent; ensure you deal with issues, rather than letting things go. Issues may otherwise build up into bigger things.
- Give plenty of warning if you are going to be late for some reason. Do not let it become a habit. Always pay a bit extra, give some time off in lieu or look at re-arranging her hours.

Traditional

- Ensure your nanny or maternity nurse likes working to a set routine.
- Recognise when a routine may have to slip a bit just to get everyone through the day.
- Make sure your nanny is happy not only to discipline or reward but, if the child is old enough, to work at making your child do the right thing the next time around.
- If you are in a hurry or pre-occupied, ensure you are not too direct or abrupt with your nanny or maternity nurse and always give praise when it is due. While she may be very experienced, she will always appreciate the praise.

> *'They have today in mind; we have the rest of our children's lives in mind. It is from a totally different perspective.'*

CHAPTER 11

Au Pairs and Mother's Helps

This chapter will take you through each step of finding an au pair or mother's help. There are additional details on au pairs and mother's helps, including pros and cons, in Chapter 3 (page 45). This chapter will help you to search, screen and interview and make that final decision.

If you are struggling with the question of whether to have live-in or live-out help, see pages 141–2 for lists of the pros and cons of each.

> 'With my au pair I made a calendar for each week of exactly what was going on and when I needed her hour by hour. It meant she could then plan her time off accordingly. She is very organised and this suited her well.'

The things you want to know first

What you can expect from them

You and your au pair or mother's help will have to agree on the details, but you can expect the following:

- Assistance with childcare.
- Sole charge of children at your discretion.
- Assistance with light domestic chores around the house and tasks such as shopping.
- Driving if you are happy with their driving ability.
- Help with your pets if they are happy to do so.

> 'If I come home and they have tidied up, I feel they are in control. I feel lighter of heart, less stressed, less pressured.'

Hours

Au pair

- An au pair on a visa generally works 25 hours a week, spread over 5 days.
- Those from an EU country and therefore not on a visa are usually on duty somewhere between 25 and 35 hours a week.
- Often an au pair works for a couple of hours in the morning and the remainder in the afternoon, leaving the middle of the day free. During this time the au pair may attend English language classes. However, it is up to you and the au pair to decide what hours and days best suit you.
- They generally expect to babysit for two evenings a week.
- They should have two free days a week.

Au pair plus

- They generally work betweeen 30 and 40 hours a week.

Mother's help

- There are no general guidelines. Some help out on a part-time basis, others work 50–55 hours a week, similar to a nanny.

Qualifications

Au pairs and mother's helps do not usually have any qualifications. However, some may have childcare qualifications or be studying for them. These are likely to be snapped up quickly!

Adult-to-child ratios

There are no set adult-to-child ratios for au pairs and mother's helps. As they are unqualified and may also be inexperienced, you need to be very realistic about what they can manage and whether they should be left in sole charge.

Costs

Au pair

Au pairs receive board, lodging and pocket money of £60–£80 per week. They should also be happy to babysit for two evenings a week, but you should pay them extra pocket money for additional babysitting or extra hours.

Au pair plus: They will expect to receive board, lodging and pocket money of £80–£110 per week. You will have to pay tax and National Insurance on anything they earn over £100 a week (see page 183).

Travelling costs: Unless you are happy to fund the travelling costs to and from the UK, an au pair will usually expect to pay these.

Language school costs: There are many free courses in the UK for EU members, but those coming from outside the EU will have to pay for their classes. If an au pair chooses to go to a private school, she usually bears the cost. It is up to you whether you offer to pay for classes or a contribution towards them.

Mother's help
Mother's helps are generally paid less than a nanny or housekeeper, approximately £130–£250 per week (net, i.e. after tax).

Special needs

Au pairs and mother's helps can be a fantastic support if your child has special needs. They are less expensive than other forms of childcare and so can give longer hours of help for the same price. However, they are unqualified so you should not leave them in sole charge of your child for any length of time unless you are totally sure of their ability. Some au pairs may not stay that long with your family – it can take time to get them up to speed and be disruptive when they leave.

> *'If using an au pair to help with a special needs child you should ensure she has good English and can understand the technical terms.'*

Searching

You have decided that you really need that extra pair of hands – well done, first major decision made! To make your search as easy as possible, follow the next few steps to work out exactly what you want in your au pair or mother's help.

Writing a job description

You may think this is totally unnecessary when all you want is someone to help out for a few hours a week. But to ensure you find the right person, she knows what to expect and you get what you want done, it is an essential step. It will help things to run much more smoothly from the start. Your job description need not be long, just a simple list of what the role entails. You can send it to prospective candidates and your final choice can agree to it before she starts. See the sample nanny job description (page 210) as a guide.

Who will suit your family?

Having worked out what you want your new au pair or mother's help to do for you, you need to think further about the characteristics and attributes you would like them to have. Think about both 'Must have' and 'Would be nice' characteristics and skills. See page 209 for a list of childcarer characteristics you may like to choose from.

Putting it all together

You should now be in a position to answer all of the headings below. This will form the basis of your search. The first table gives an example of how you might fill in the information.

What	Mother's help.
When	Three mornings a week and two afternoons.
For whom	A 3-year-old boy and 18-month-old girl, new baby due.
Where	Central London.
Main duties	Shared charge, occasional sole charge of two older children, light housework.
Skills needed	Driver, able to cook simple dishes, previous experience with children.
Characteristics	Cheerful, caring, reliable, lots of initiative.

What	
When	
For whom	
Where	
Main duties	
Skills needed	
Characteristics	

The main search options

Different people have different ways of doing things. Some would rather use an agency, others would rather save money and remain more in control by using a website or magazine ad. Others prefer only to find people via word of mouth.

'State exactly what you are looking for, and look hard for the perfect match.'

Agencies

There are now hundreds of au pair and home help agencies offering to find the right person for you. See page 145 for the pros and cons of agencies, followed by ideas on finding a good one and getting the best out of them.

However, remember that au pair agencies are slightly different in that they may not have met their candidates. Nonetheless, they should have a good network in the countries they are sourcing au pairs from and a good agency should not be recommending someone they do not think is up to the job. For your peace of mind you will need to ensure you interview candidates thoroughly and check references properly, but the agency should be able to give invaluable help at every point, particularly on the important subject of visas. Au pair agencies usually offer very good service in terms of finding another au pair if your first one does not work out within a certain probationary period.

While there are few industry standards, it is a good sign if the agency is a member of the Bristish Au Pair Agencies Association (BAPAA). They have a list of member agencies on their website (bapaa.org.uk). They also have a search facility on their site that enables any au pair employed through a BAPAA-registered agency to search for other au pairs in her area – a great way for your new au pair to start a social life when she arrives.

'You get those who really want to come to learn the language and be here for the right reasons, not just to earn money and with no real interest in children.'

Websites

These can be a fantastic source for finding someone, but there is a bit of time and effort involved. See page 148 for the pros and cons of using websites to find an employee.

General community websites
These have ads for almost anything you can imagine from flat shares to cars for sale. They list jobs as well as details of people looking for jobs. The most well known in the UK is gumtree.com. Depending on the site, it may be free to display your ad or you may have to pay a fee of approximately £20.

Specialised community websites
These are like the community websites but they specialise in childcare. They will have families offering jobs and childcarers offering their services. They may be attached to a parenting or childcare information or discussion website. A family is usually charged between £10 and £30 to post an ad. For example, nannyjob.co.uk, greatcare.co.uk and nannyselect.co.uk all allow you to look for au pairs and mother's helps as well as nannies.

Au pair specialised matching websites
These operate like an introductory or dating website. You put up the details of your family, the job and the type of person you are looking for. Au pairs do the same and then you can each look at what is available and suits your criteria. You can make initial contact through the site, but the rest is then up to you. You need to be prepared for a lot of sifting and email writing as you can receive quite a number of responses every day. Generally you can search for free but you have to pay a membership fee to post your details or contact an au pair. Examples of sites include: greataupair.com and aupair-world.net.

Posting your website ad
Before you post an ad, look through other ads to get an idea of what people are saying and what you think works well. With so many families looking for help, you need to try to make your ad stand out from the crowd and be appealing without sounding too whacky or desperate. Try to include a photo of you and your children.

Beware! Though they are few and far between, there are people who operate scams through these sites either to get a visa into the country or to get you to send them money. Never send money to an au pair before she starts and always check references before starting the visa process.

Magazines

Placing ads in magazines has dipped in popularity as the internet is such a popular medium. However, most of the relevant magazines now have jobs listed in the magazine and on job boards on their website. These are more suited to finding a mother's help than an au pair, particularly a more experienced mother's help. Also, if you want a mother's help with certain skills, for example, a mother's help/groom, you can advertise in a magazine that is dedicated to that area. See page 149 for the pros and cons of using magazines to search for childcare, page 211 for an example of an ad for a nanny and page 220 for details of magazines in which you might advertise.

Other places for ads

You can also place ads:

- In local shops.
- On community notice boards.
- At childcare training colleges.

The pros and cons are similar to those associated with magazine ads.

Word of mouth

Some people are only happy if they find someone via word of mouth, while others see it as a sure way to ruin a friendship. If using this method to find childcare, make sure you are very specific about what you want. You may like to send out an email so that people can then forward it to their friends. See page 150 for the pros and cons of searching by word of mouth.

Someone from abroad

You may find an au pair or a foreign mother's help who sounds absolutely ideal, but then discover that getting her a visa will be exceptionally difficult. It pays to be aware of which nationalities find it easier to gain entrance to the UK.

- Anyone from the EU can automatically enter the UK and work here.
- Anyone from a country that operates within the UK au pair scheme (see bia.homeoffice.gov.uk or ukvisas.gov.uk for details) is able to enter as an au pair, although criteria need to be met and a visa may be needed. It seems likely that the dedicated Au Pair Visa will cease to exist for most countries and be replaced with a Youth Mobility Visa.

- Anyone from Commonwealth countries that offer Working Holiday Visas can enter the UK and work as an au pair, though they need to meet the necessary criteria.

There are other things to consider as well, for example anyone from Australia, New Zealand, South Africa, the USA or Canada will be able to speak good English. Those from South Africa, Australia and New Zealand will be used to driving on the left. You may, however, prefer that someone brings a new language and culture into your home.

> *'Having an au pair is like having another child and takes lots of management at the beginning.'*

Always check visa requirements as you can spend a lot of time sorting out a visa for someone only to find that they are not eligible for it, they decide not to come, or they arrive in the country but never arrive in your home. Also never, ever send money to anyone before they start working for you.

> *'It works well when they get good guidance – it is having the time to do it. If I have a good day it is fine, if I am having a bad day, then it all goes wrong.'*

Screening

Creating an assessment sheet

Work out a simple system to assess people during your search and interviews. You could use the assessment sheet on page 212 (you can make copies of this sheet so that you have one for each candidate) or alter this sheet so that it suits you better. (See page 143 and page 209 for examples of 'must have' and 'would be nice' characteristics and skills.) It can be helpful to put stars next to points you think are particularly important, or question marks next to things that worry you. Where possible, make sure you check relevant documentation, for example, proof of identity and any relevant qualifications.

Use your initial screening to get three or four candidates for either a telephone or face-to-face interview, depending on their location.

Making a shortlist

Go through your prospective candidates and screen them into groups of Yes, No and Maybe. Be strict with your screening as you do not want to waste their time or yours.

- **Yes:** Communicate with them further to find out a bit more about each other. It is important that you both have all the necessary information before deciding to go forward to a more in-depth interview.

> **Important note:** Always give a realistic and measured overview of the role and your family. Do not oversell the job as someone will arrive, be disappointed, become unmotivated and probably leave.

- **No:** Tell them no, sooner rather than later. Always take the time to thank people for their application and to let them know you will not be taking things further.
- **Maybe:** If you can, keep on hold those who nearly fit the bill.

Interviewing

While people find being interviewed quite nerve racking, they don't often pause to think that the interviewer might be more nervous than them! Preparing well will help you to feel calmer. Remember, a candidate will always look to you to take control.

If you are interviewing people from abroad you may only have the chance to interview them by phone. When interviewing an au pair you should be less challenging than with a nanny or mother's help. You are interviewing someone to join your family and help out rather than for a professional job. Below are some tips for interviewing by telephone. See page 152 for information on interviewing face to face.

Interviewing by telephone

- Ensure you pre-arrange a time to call, via email or your agency depending on how you are searching, and also ensure she knows approximately how long the interview will last, for example, 20–30 minutes.
- Check you have the right phone number and country code and that you will not be disturbed during the call. Always ensure you call at the time you said you would.
- Start the interview by asking how she is and other small talk to help put you both at ease. Thank her for putting aside the time to talk to you. Try to remain as as at ease and friendly as you can – you will get more from your candidate and a better sense of who she is.

- Let her know the structure of the interview, for example, that you will outline the job, then ask some questions and then allow her to ask you some questions.
- Do not be afraid to get her to repeat herself or clarify something. Ask additional clarifying questions to ensure you get all the information you need.
- You may be surprised at how bad her English sounds but remember she is likely to be out of practice and will find it much harder to speak English on the phone, rather than face to face.
- If you are having trouble making up your mind, don't be afraid to conduct a second or third interview by phone and get your partner to conduct a telephone interview with her too.

Interview structure and questions

Plan this in advance. Make notes as you go through the interview; you may like to use a scoring system, for example:

3 = ideal/above requirements

2 = adequate

1 = below requirements/needs development

You can then transfer the key points and the scores onto your assessment sheets.

Here are some suggestions for structuring an interview:

The role
Concisely explain the nature of the role. You may like to include additional details such as:

- How much or how little you and/or your partner will be around.
- What the accommodation you are offering is like and whether there is phone or internet access in her room.
- Rules for use of the car and any house rules you feel she might take exception to.
- Details of any pets.
- Benefits to her, such as other au pairs, mother's helps or nannies in the area, any perks of the job and of the area.
- How you like to work with your childcarer.

Remember to be honest and not give unrealistic expectations of the job.

The person

Review her CV and experience. Always ensure you have a copy of anything she has sent you. Don't just say 'Tell me about yourself'.

- Ask relevant questions about the areas that interest you, or any gaps you are worried about.
- Find out what elements she particularly liked or disliked about previous work and/or education.
- Ask about reasons for leaving jobs or doing particular courses.
- Ask her if there is anything else she would like to add.

Additional questions

It is important to have a list of prepared questions. You should try to ask questions around the qualities you are interested in. To give you a few ideas, here are some of the more common questions that people ask.

> *'Make sure your au pair genuinely likes and wants to spend time with children.'*

Au pair/mother's help questions

- What is it about being an au pair/mother's help that appeals to you?
- What is it about being in the UK that particularly appeals to you?
- What do you like about working with children?
- What characteristics do you have that you think help you work well with children?
- What are you proud of having achieved in your life/in your last job?
- Have you been involved in an emergency situation with a child? If so, what happened and how did you deal with it?
- What sorts of activities would you do with my children?
- Do you enjoy cooking? What sort of meals would you prepare for my children?
- Have you got any medical history I should be aware of?
- Why are you particularly interested in this family?
- What characteristics are you looking for in an employer/a family?
- What are your long-term goals?
- Would I be able to contact your referees by phone? When would be convenient?
- Have you been to the UK before? Do you know anyone in the UK/this area?

See page 154 for additional questions that you may also like to ask.

For an au pair couple

- How long have you been together? Where did you meet?
- How do you prefer to work together? Have you had any problems working together?
- How do you think you complement each other?
- Do you go home on holiday at the same time?

Payment and benefits

When you feel you have gathered enough information, talk about payment or pocket money and additional benefits. If the candidate has interviewed well make sure she is clear on:

- Pay or pocket money.
- Hours.
- Time off.
- Holiday entitlement.
- Car use.
- Phone and internet use.
- Amount of sole charge, if any.
- Live-in details.

Holiday entitlement

For mother's helps the statutory minimum for paid holiday is 28 days a year including Bank Holidays (from 1 October 2008).

An au pair is entitled to a minimum of two weeks' holiday per year, although most families will give between three and four weeks. An au pair should still be paid pocket money when on holiday.

Other benefits

The benefits you offer to an au pair can make a big difference to her pocket. If she already has a mobile phone you should provide a weekly or monthly contribution to this or provide a pay-as-you-go phone. Keep your au pair's spirits up and your landline bills down by providing access to the internet/Skype or cheap phonecards to keep in contact with home. If providing a car, you may like to agree a weekly or monthly petrol allowance above what she will use during the course of her work.

Wrapping up

Don't give an answer at the end of the interview. You need time to think about everything you have heard and also to think of anything you may have missed out. Thank her for her time and say when you will contact her. Don't be afraid to say you are interviewing other people.

Making up your mind

Always keep track of who you have seen and what you thought of them. You may find that you have an outright winner. If not, the fact that you have taken a systematic approach should pay off. Look at the sheets from the interviews. Who has the most positive points? Who did you feel right about? It is important that you use both your head and heart – not just one or the other.

> *'It can go really well if you have the same mindset as the other person.'*

Second interview or short-term trial

If they are in the UK, you may like to ask your shortlist, or just your favoured candidate, back for a second time and even a short-term trial. This will help you to make up your mind or confirm you have made the right decision. A second interview should be longer and more relaxed, for example over two hours, half a day or longer. This will allow the candidate to spend time with the children and see how your household works. If relevant, come to a suitable financial arrangement. If your partner has not already done so, get him to meet her or interview her on the phone.

Offering the job

Hopefully, when you offer the job or au pair placement, your chosen candidate will say yes! However, do be prepared for her to say she has decided that it is not the right job for her. It is probably not a good idea to try to persuade her otherwise. You want someone who is keen, not someone you have had to beg.

Quick tip: If your prospective au pair or mother's help wants more money than you are offering and you feel you cannot stretch that far, you could offer additional time off, a pay review after three or six months or some other benefit.

Once someone has accepted your job offer, you need to breathe a sigh of relief and then check references (see page 179) and, for a UK citizen, carry out a Criminal Records Bureau check (see page 180). If your childcarer is coming from abroad, you could get a check done in that country – these are often referred to as Certificates of Good Conduct. Be prepared for this taking both time and effort. If you are using an agency, they should be able to do this for you.

Tips for your parenting style

Following on from the questionnaire in Chapter 1 (see page 23), here are some tips and ideas for working with au pairs and mother's helps for each of the styles. You should take note of the points for your stronger style(s), or you may like to read through all of them!

> *'Let her know what your style is, what kind of person you are. Find out what her strengths are, and build on them.'*

Keep them safe

- Find out what her safety and first-aid knowledge is like and ensure she knows all the basics, and where the first-aid kit and list of emergency numbers are. Make sure she is aware of your particular safety worries and conscious of things such as shutting doors and safety gates, and keeping hot and sharp things away from small grabbing hands.
- For her to be of maximum use to you and to enjoy her job and increase her skills, you should hand over progressively more responsibility to her. Tell and show her what to do, then let her get on with it. This may be difficult for you to do, but you can't build your trust in her if you don't.
- She may have been brought up very differently from you and may not have the same cleaning and food-preparation standards as you. Explain your way of doing things and your reasons. Help her to put these into practice, rather than sneaking round after her, or visibly doing it yourself, as this will only undermine her.

Freedom

- Ensure you invest enough time to get your au pair or mother's help up to speed otherwise she could feel rather at sea, and the children could potentially be getting away with more than they should.
- You will have experienced a steep learning curve when you first had a baby, and she may be going through something similar if she does not have much childcare experience. Pace out what she needs to learn over time so she is not too overloaded and ensure she understands everything. Monitor and praise her efforts.

- Remember not to become overly friendly. A blurring of boundaries can make things difficult.
- Ensure you tackle issues as they arise rather than letting things go as this could cause resentment to build up on either side.

Traditional

- Ensure you are very clear about the daily routine and what help you need from her at which points in the day. If she does not have much childcare experience she may not understand the importance you place on routines.
- You may like to map out progress milestones for her for each month or six weeks.
- Ensure you show her how you would prefer that she disciplined your child – she may have been brought up very differently from you. Give her praise when she does it properly – it can be very daunting disciplining someone's child in front of them. Resist the temptation to wade in and do it yourself.
- Ensure you are not too direct or abrupt with her when you feel things are not running as they should. She will be trying hard and it may take a bit of time to get into the swing of it, particularly if her English is not very good.

Part 4

Working with Your Childcare

CHAPTER 12

Finances, References and Contracts

Financial help

According to your financial position and the type of childcare that you are using, you may be able to claim financial help from the Government.

Tax Credits and Working Tax Credits

You may be able to claim Child Tax Credits from the Government if you have at least one child who lives with you. The majority of families within the UK will qualify, but dependent on circumstances, different amounts will be received.

You may also be eligible for Working Tax Credits if you work but earn below a certain amount. This can be claimed whether you are employed or self-employed and you may get more if you pay for childcare.

Both Child Tax Credits and Working Tax Credits will be paid directly into your bank account.

To find out more details and if you are eligible call 0845 300 3900 or go to http://taxcredits.direct.gov.uk.

Childcare Vouchers

Some companies run a Childcare Voucher Scheme. You are not eligible for Childcare Vouchers if you are self-employed or are not working.

Employers offer these as a benefit to their staff, who will not have to pay tax or National Insurance Contributions on the vouchers and can therefore save up to £1196 per year. If both parents use this scheme a family can save up to £2392. Employers also make National Insurance savings themselves.

Registered childcare

In order for you to claim the childcare element of Working Tax Credits and employer-supported Childcare Vouchers, the childcare must be registered with the Government. Most types of registered childcare are included: childminders, nurseries (day, work and pre-school), out-of-school clubs, holiday clubs and nannies registered through the Voluntary Childcare Register. Check with the childcare provider that they are Government registered. If you are paying a friend, you may be able to claim as long as your friend is happy to register as a childminder or nanny, under the Voluntary Childcare Register. If you are paying a relative, he or she would have to become a registered childminder. As a childminder, your relative or friend would have to look after additional children and would need to childmind in his or her own home rather than yours.

For more information speak to your employer or go to the Inland Revenue site (hmrc.gov.uk/childcare) or the Daycare Trust site (daycaretrust.org.uk).

Early years funding

The Government offers up to five free sessions a week (for up to 38 weeks of the year) of pre-school education for children over 3 years of age, although there are some variations depending on where you are in the UK. This is also being extended to 2-year-olds in some disadvantaged areas. Sessions are usually for 2½ or 3 hours. If your child is attending childcare for longer than the time allocated in the five sessions, the cost of the five sessions will be deducted from your fees.

All day nurseries, nursery schools, pre-schools, playgroups (and now childminders in England and Wales), which are registered as an Early Education Provider, can offer the sessions. For further details talk to your local Children's Information Service, visit the Childlink website (childlink.gov.uk), or talk to the childcare provider themselves. In Northern Ireland talk to your local Health and Social Services Trust.

University and college discounts and subsidies

Some university and college nurseries offer a discount in your nursery fees if you are a student or employee. Some have nursery subsidies for undergraduate and postgraduate students. These, however, are likely to be limited and dependent on income. Talk to your university or college nursery for further information.

References (out-of-home options)

Do not be afraid to ask your preferred childcare provider about obtaining references from other parents. If they provide a good service they should be happy to do this. If you can, check them by phone. This is quicker and easier for everyone and gives a better idea of what the referee thinks. Ask questions about the areas you are interested in or worried about. The questions below are relevant to all types of childcare, and are followed by extra questions that are relevant to particular types of provider:

- Would you recommend .... ? Why?
- Are they safety minded? Could you give me an example of this?
- What do you feel your children particularly like about .... ?
- Did you feel that they passed on enough information about your child's day to you? Or any worries they had about them?
- Was there anything you felt they could have done better?

Day nursery, work nursery and crèche questions

- Did you feel your child got enough individual attention?
- What do you think about the calibre of the staff?

Nursery/pre-school questions

- Did you feel your child got enough individual attention?
- What do you think about the calibre of the staff?
- Did you feel they made learning fun?

Out-of-school care questions

- Did you feel your child was learning as much as they should?
- Did you feel that they had a good range of activities?
- Did you feel that your children had time to rest and recharge? Did you feel they got overtired or over-stimulated?
- Did you feel your child got enough individual attention?
- What do you think about the calibre of the staff?

References (in-home options)

'Don't rely on paper – you must talk to people.'

Always, always check references – it is amazing the number of people who don't! If you can, check them by phone. This is quicker and gives a better idea of what the referee thinks. You can detect nuances in their voice and ask specific questions. Some au pairs, in particular, may not have worked in this capacity before, so you will have to ask the referee how they know her and alter the questions accordingly. For an au pair from abroad you may need to find someone who speaks the appropriate language to carry out the checks either by phone or email. Some questions you might like to use are detailed below. Ask them around the areas you are interested in or worried about:

- Would you recommend Suzy as an au pair/nanny/nanny-housekeeper? Why?
- Would you say she is safety minded? Could you give me an example of this?
- What is her cooking like?'
- Is she an easy person to have in your house/get along with?
- Was there anything you felt she could have done better?
- How did your children get on with her? Could you give me an example?
- If she was your au pair/nanny again what would you do differently?

   'I checked her school website to ascertain she was who she said she was and that her referee really was a teacher there. It all checked out which made me feel a lot better and increased my confidence about the whole thing.'

Criminal Records Bureau (CRB) check

With no national register for in-home childcare in the UK you may want to get a Criminal Records Bureau check done. If you are using an agency, they should do it for you. For you to carry out a check you need to use an umbrella body or company, which will do all the paperwork for you at a small cost – see the Government website crb.gov.uk for details.

   If you would rather not carry out reference and CRB checks yourself there are companies who can do everything for you, for example, Nanny Check (nanny-check.co.uk).

Contracts

According to the type of childcare provider you choose, you may have to sign a contract or put one together for both you and the provider to sign.

Nurseries

Most nurseries will ask you to sign a contract before your child starts. They may also ask to see proof of your identity, for example, a passport or driving licence and for a copy of your child's birth certificate.

> *'Our nursery's form asked if we would like to be told if our child takes his first step while in their care, or if we rather they pretended it hadn't happened with them. It shows that they know what is important to you.'*

The contract may cover the following:

- All contact and collection details.
- Weekly or monthly hours.
- Costs, including those for late collection or additional time.
- Payment details: how often, whether in advance or arrears and by what method.
- Food: who will provide it and what is expected.
- Holiday and sickness arrangements, including notice periods and charges.
- Notice needed to change sessions or days attended.
- Notice needed of giving up your nursery place.
- Important details about your child, for example, allergies, medicines, doctor's number, special routines or toys.

Crèches

A crèche is unlikely to ask for so much detail; however, they will take all your contact details as well as details about your child's likes, dislikes and any medical information.

Nursery schools and pre-schools

Nursery schools and pre-schools may have a detailed contract, or may have a simple form which asks for your contact details, your child's likes and dislikes and any medical history or allergies.

Childminders

You should always agree a childminding contract before your children start. This will protect both you and your childminder and ensure you both have the same expectations. Your childminder will probably have a standard contract. If not, they can be bought from the NCMA website (ncma.org.uk).

It should cover:

- All contact and collection details.
- Weekly or monthly hours.
- Costs, including those for late collection or additional time.
- Payment details: how often and by what method.
- Food: who will provide it and what is expected.
- Car usage and outings: permission for your childminder to take your child in the car and to playgroups or other activities.
- Holiday and sickness arrangements, including notice periods and charges.
- Important details for your child, for example, allergies, medicines, doctor's number, special routines or toys.

Out-of-school care

Most out-of-school care will have a simple agreement form, which asks for your contact details and particular details about your child. Some may have more detailed contracts relating to particular activities.

Nannies and mother's helps

To protect both you and your employee you should draw up a contract or agreement and both sign it before they start. See page 213 for an example of a nanny contract. Always add in extra details of the job you feel you would like to be in writing. If appropriate, the contract should stipulate that it will still stand should you have any further children. (You should, if possible, give a pay rise when an additional child comes along as it will obviously increase the workload.)

'Have a very clear contract that covers everything.'

Maternity nurses and night nannies

A contract with a maternity nurse or night nanny will generally be shorter and be more of a working agreement. It should include details of duties, hours, days off and length of contract, pay and notice needed to terminate the contract.

Au pairs

You do not need to draw up a contract for an au pair or au pair plus – a simple agreement document or offer letter will suffice. This avoids confusion and protects both you and your au pair. It does not need to be as detailed as a contract but should include details of the job, pocket money (including petrol and phone contributions), hours (including babysitting) and holiday entitlement.

You may also have to help your au pair to secure her visa. She may need a letter of invitation from you and proof of your identity. Generally an au pair pays for her own flight to the country, although you may like to make a contribution when she arrives with you. Never send money to an unknown au pair.

Your responsibilities as an employer

Tax and National Insurance

As maternity nurses and night nannies are self-employed you do not have to worry about their tax, but if you employ a nanny, a nanny-housekeeper or a mother's help in the UK, by law, you are responsible for paying their tax and National Insurance. This includes filing their annual tax return. Failure to do this will result in penalties.

You need to register as a new employer with the Inland Revenue (hmrc.gov.uk). They will then send you all the necessary details for operating your payroll. It does not take too much time and effort, but it does take a bit, particularly to get started. There are an abundance of agencies that can be found on the internet which will take over all your payroll responsibilities for a fixed yearly fee of anything from £90 to £300.

Whether you decide to operate your own payroll or pay someone to do it for you, your new nanny should give you her P45 form. This summarises her pay and tax to date in the current tax year. It will also give you her National Insurance number.

Insurance

The majority of household policies will cover employer's liability for domestic staff, but you should check your policy to make sure. Some nannies also take out their own cover.

If your childcarer will be driving your children, ensure they have the appropriate cover.

Au pairs

You are not liable to pay any tax on money paid to an au pair or an au pair plus, unless you are paying her over £100 per week. You do, however, have a duty of care. You should make her feel at home and always, always ensure she is given her pocket money, including petrol, phone and overtime money on time. Ensure she understands and takes her full holiday entitlement. The more care you take to ensure your au pair is happy, the longer she is likely to stay.

EU au pairs and those on au pair visas are entitled to use the National Health Service, but may want to take out additional travel insurance to cover their belongings, etc. Those on other visas will have to pay for their healthcare or may wish to take out health insurance as well as additional travel insurance, if they do not have it already.

If your au pair is going to be driving, ensure the car is safe and properly insured. It is wise to pay for an au pair to have a couple of lessons.

Where possible, try to pick your au pair up from her point of arrival into the country, be it an airport, bus or train station.

CHAPTER 13

Making It Work and Solving Problems

Making it work (out-of-home options)

Choosing the childcare that is best for you and your children has taken both time and effort, so it makes sense to ensure that your relationship with your childcarer works. Follow these five steps to make a success of your out-of-home childcare.

1 Know what to expect

Ensure that you are very clear on the service and care that your childcare provider offers. While most expectations will be laid out in your contract, it is sometimes the smaller things that can cause misunderstandings:

- Ensure you and the provider are each clear on your day-to-day responsibilities: food, nappies, changes of clothes, car seats, pick-ups, drop-offs, etc.

    'It can be quite frustrating when parents consistently don't send in the right things, like nappies, formula and spare clothes.' – Natalie, nursery manager

- Ensure you understand and are happy with the routine your child will be following. This includes the educational format at a nursery school or pre-school and the activities and structure at an out-of-school club.

- If your child is at potty-training age, ensure you understand what the childcarer will and will not do to help make this successful.
- Ask at the beginning if there is anything the provider would particularly like from you, for example, no prolonged goodbyes when you drop off your child, written notification of holidays.

Crèches

- If using a crèche at a leisure or shopping centre, remember that it is your responsibility to return as quickly as possible if they call you to come back and see your child.

Nursery schools and pre-schools

- While they are still very much a form of childcare, nursery schools and pre-schools operate along the same principles as a school and expect you to understand this.

  'It was more structured than I thought. They have strict pick-up and drop-off times to get them ready for school. I had to make a real effort to get myself more organised in the mornings to get there on time!'

- Make sure that you fully understand what a pre-school requires from you in terms of support and involvement from parents.

  'If they are unable to assist with the sessions on a regular basis, they may be able to do some fundraising, help with the nativity costumes, or if they have a particular skill, come and share it with the children.' – Ann, pre-school supervisor

Childminders

- Ensure that a childminder fully understands your child's routine.
- Be clear if you, or your child, like things done in a certain way. Let her know what your rules are, for example, no sweets, limited TV.

Out-of-school care

- Remember that an out-of-school club does not give formal schooling and may not be prepared to help your child with homework.

  'We aim to be fun and educational at the same time, rather than babysitters. We work to inspire and encourage children.' – Anna-Kate, out-of-school and holiday club provider

2 Settle your child in

You want your childcare arrangement to start well, so it is vital to take time to settle your child in happily. Here are some ideas:

- If this is the first time your child has been away from you for any length of time, try to settle him or her in gradually and gently.
- If you are returning to work, start taking your child a week or two early and leave them for short sessions to begin with. Gradually increase the time they spend there. You may want to stay for the entirety of the first visit.
- If you are unable to arrange any settling-in sessions, you may like to get your child to spend some time with a friend or relative, to get them used to being apart from you.
- If you know another child who attends the childcare setting, and your child is old enough, arrange a couple of play-dates. A familiar face on the first day can really make a difference, particularly for a shy child.
- If you are very worried about settling your child in, talk to your child's carer. They will probably have dealt with similar situations to yours and be able to put your mind at rest. Confirm that younger children can bring in a toy or comforter with them.

  'My son always settled better if he could bring something in from home.'

- If your child is old enough, talk openly and excitedly about going to childcare. There are also books available which tell a story about starting nursery or nursery school. If you talk about it the night before, your child will know to expect it in the morning.

  'It can help if they come in with a purpose. Bring a carrot from home for the guinea pigs.' – Lucinda, nursery school head

- To get off to a good start, ensure you get into a routine of early bed times and calm mornings. A new environment, new toys and new friends can be very tiring. If attending a breakfast club, this is important as a flustered start to every day is likely to mean a longer settling-in period.
- When dropping off on your first day ensure all your arrangements have been finalised, for example, payment and contact information. This means that you can really focus on your child. Greet the staff/childcarer warmly to show your child that you like and trust them.
- When it is time to leave, give your child a warm goodbye and then leave straight away; make sure they see you leave. If they start crying do not come back; this is what they want and all it will do is make it upsetting for both of you, and ultimately harder for them to settle.

  'Just go, don't hang round – it only upsets the child more.' – Jennifer, nursery key worker

- You may like to phone after an hour or so on the first couple of days to check on progress. But do not make a habit of it and do not phone throughout the day.
- If you have a shy child, ensure you arrive early. As other children arrive they will then go to join your child. If you arrive later than the majority of other children your child will have to go and join a seemingly intimidating group.
- Remember that it can take a child six to eight weeks to settle (a few weeks at out-of-school care).

> *'It is often the mother you are settling in. They need to be confident that this is the right place for their child. If she isn't comfortable with it, then the child won't be.' – Lucinda, nursery school head*

Day nurseries and work nurseries

Day nurseries can be hard for children to settle into as they are very different from a home setting. Additionally, your child may be quite young and may not have been separated from you much in the past. In September 2005 Cambridge University and the Free University of Berlin reported that in the first few days of nursery a child's stress level can be 75 to 100 per cent higher than at home. However, do also bear in mind that nurseries are designed specifically for your child's age and have trained and experienced staff who will have successfully settled in many children.

> *'We always treat every child as an individual when settling them in.' – Susan, pre-school assistant*

Nursery schools and pre-schools

When it comes to a nursery school or pre-school, some children take to it like ducks to water, particularly if they have older siblings. As they are a bit older, they may have already experienced other forms of childcare. They understand that it is a grown-up thing to be going to school and it makes them feel proud and independent – this transition can sometimes be harder for the parent than the child!

- Some nursery schools and pre-schools run a weekly settling-in session, the term before your child is due to start, for children and their parents. You can take your child along to get used to the setting, the teacher and the other children who will be attending – all with you there.

> *'We encourage mums to come, but also to pop to the shops for 10 minutes, so the child learns that you will go, but you will also come back.' – Ann, pre-school supervisor*

- A nursery school will be happy for you to stay for a while during the first few sessions but are likely to want you to start leaving your child sooner rather than later. Talk to the school and work out a plan. If you do stay for a time, ensure you let your child get to know the teacher and classroom assistant and try to melt into the background.

- You can usually attend pre-school sessions but should try to leave your child to get on with things as soon as possible.

Out-of-school care

Some children will take a bit of time to settle into out-of-school care. It can make for a long day particularly if they are young and getting used to school as well. Others will settle in easily as they are usually centred around play and fun. If you are worried about your child's reaction, do remember that the staff are trained and will have settled in many children in the past.

- You may like to try to settle your child in gently by starting them with just one or two sessions a week and gradually working your way up. If you are working full time a friend or relative may be able to help put this plan into action.
- After the first session, talk to the play workers and find out how your child got on.

3 Communicate

This is the basis of working well with any form of childcare. In a busy nursery, crèche, nursery school or pre-school, when your only point of face-to-face communication is at the busy drop-off and pick-up times, communication can be rushed or overlooked. There may also be little time when dropping off or picking up at a childminder's.

- Think about what you and your childcare provider need to know on a daily basis.
- Leave home a bit earlier if you have something important to say, or stay a bit later when you pick up and everyone is not so stressed.
- If you think you will forget something, write a quick and cheerful note the night before and give it to your child's carer.
- Communicate succinctly and clearly so that even if it is a busy time, your childcarer will take on board what you are saying. If you feel it is too busy, ask when would be a good time to have a quick discussion.
- Do tell them if things are not quite right with your child on a particular day, for example, if they have had a bad night's sleep or something else you feel might throw them off course. It will make the day easier for both your child and their carer.

> *'It is difficult when they don't tell you the child has been ill the night before. I can see it from a parent's point of view that sometimes work does have to come first. It would help if they could see it from mine – I don't want to add to their hassles, but I do need the information to help me do my job well.' – Becky, childminder*

- At a nursery, nursery school or pre-school, you may always race past the notice board as you dash to work, or feel your child gets returned to you with too many bits of paper – but these contain vital communication. Do try to read them and act on them.
- Ensure you are open and receptive to what your childcarer is telling you.
- Remember that working in a nursery, nursery school or pre-school is a busy, and at times, stressful job and that childminding can be quite an isolating job. Give praise when it is due – it can make a big difference to someone's day. Share with them the sweet or funny things that your child says about them to you.

Day nurseries and work nurseries
- If your nursery uses a record book to let you know about your child's day and on-going development, you can also use it to communicate with the nursery.

> *'Both the nursery and parent fills in the record book. As a first-time mum it was great to know his routine was being followed and what he got up to during the day. As I could write comments in it about his night and his needs for that day, I could dump and run in the mornings.'*

Nursery schools and pre-schools
- Always try to attend parents' evenings at nursery school or pre-school as this gives you a dedicated slot to discuss your child's progress and anything you are concerned about.

> *'It is very weird going to parents' evening. You don't feel old enough and you don't feel your child is old enough. You feel you won't have enough to talk about, they are only 3 after all – and then you can't stop!'*

Childminders
- Be careful to manage boundaries with a childminder. If you get to know each other too well it may be hard to raise issues or problems.

4 Ensure your child is happy

You will not be happy with your choice of childcare unless your child is. You know your child better than anyone else and need to assess how well he or she is settling in. However, do remember that a child will generally plump for a parent over anything else and may pull every stunt in the book to get their preference. If you are concerned:

- Turn up early or unannounced and assess whether things are running as smoothly as you would hope and how your child is when you are not there or expected.
- Note if your child is behaving differently – more withdrawn, clingy or aggressive. Are there any unexplained bruises or cuts? Do they make any comments that worry you?
- Note whether your childcarer seems aware of your child's feelings.
- Talk to the childcarer and see what their thoughts are on the situation and what ideas they come up with to try to settle your child in better.
- You may want to re-arrange the sessions so your child spends more time with children he or she likes (or you think he or she would like if they haven't met). Or, for some types of childcare, you could try cutting back on the sessions so they only go once or twice a week and then increase them again, once they are more settled.
- If you know another parent who uses or has used the same childcarer, you may want to talk to them and see if they have any suggestions.

If you do have concerns, it is vitally important that you talk to your child and the childcarer and listen to what they both say – however, the final decision will rest with you. Your child may just need a bit more time to get settled, or a different childcarer or a different type of childcare might need to be considered.

5 Don't take them for granted

Good childcare is in demand, so protect your place (and places for possible future children!) by working well with them. Always treat the childcarer with respect and courtesy; remember they are doing a very important job.

- Ensure you drop off and pick up on time.
- Give plenty of warning if plans change.
- Always, always pay your provider on time, or ensure your Childcare Vouchers reach them on time.
- Take time to get to know your provider as an individual and build up a good working relationship.

Nursery schools and pre-schools

- Remember that a nursery school or pre-school is run as a school and will want your child there for the beginning of the session. Try to not let your child miss too many of their sessions in the term-time. Although the children are under the age of having to attend by law, you do not want them to feel they are behind the others.

Childminders

- Keep the relationship professional, yet friendly. It will make it easier to deal with the ups and downs.

Out-of-school care

- An out-of-school club may not be formally educating your child, but they are nurturing and caring for your child, and he or she may spend quite a bit of the week with them – don't see them as some sort of holding zone for your child.
- Always thank staff at an out-of-school club for their efforts – they will be putting in long hours too.

Making it work (in-home options)

In-home childcare needs careful management. Here are five steps to make a success of your chosen childcare. Alternatively, nannysuccess.com can compile an affordable, tailored plan to help you manage your nanny, au pair or housekeeper in a way that best suits your personality.

1 Put pen to paper

Writing things down enables your childcarer to know what her responsibilities are and how you prefer things to be done – fewer issues should then arise.

You may like to write down the following:

- Your children's daily routine.

   'I have a weekly plan and I run through what we need to achieve each day, for example, the kitchen tidied in the morning, the washing done, the chickens fed, help painting the bathroom. I always write it down.'

- Important information, for example, any allergies, location of first aid kit, emergency numbers.
- The things you feel strongly about, for example, discipline, TV, table manners, sweets, blankets or comfort toys, dummies, etc.

- Specific information relating to each child, for example, favourite toys, bed-time rituals.

Friends and relatives
It might seem unnecessary for a relative or friend, but writing important information down will help avoid confusion and awkward situations. It will create a few rules and boundaries and will also help him or her to pick things up faster and do things the way you prefer.

- You should write down the principles of how you will work as a sign of respect to each other, including hours, giving notice of change of plans, holidays, time off, payment or other recompense. Ensure your friend or relative has an opportunity to add their own thoughts to this, and that you are coming to a mutual agreement that both parties are happy with.

   'My mum would turn up at 9.15 instead of 9am. As it is not as formal, you can't say anything as they are helping you out, so you just sit and stew.'

Nannies
- Start with a clear job description (see page 210 for an example).
- If you are involved in a nanny share, you will need to work with the other family from the start and write down the points you agree upon. Write down how you will split the start-up costs, salary, tax, insurance, groceries, travel, overtime, holiday pay and any future pay rise.

Au pairs and mother's helps
- Start with a clear job description (see page 210 for an example).
- If an au pair is very inexperienced, you will need to explain everything in great detail. You will be surprised by how much baby and childcare knowledge you have soaked up.
- Include important safety rules (particularly if employing an inexperienced au pair).

   'She had no idea a 3-year-old should not use scissors. She has never been around children. When she goes out, she leaves the front door ajar.'

- There may be language difficulties. If things are written down your au pair can use a foreign-language-to-English dictionary to translate words she is not sure of. You may also have to show her how to do certain things or give extra time and guidance.

   'We had a Brazilian au pair and we kept a Portuguese to English dictionary in the kitchen. It really helped over the first few weeks.'

2 Set boundaries

Boundaries are probably not such an issue for a **friend** or **relative** as these will depend on your existing relationship. For **nannies** and **au pairs**, however, setting clear rules and boundaries makes things easier for everyone – particularly if you will be at home a lot, working or otherwise. It is important to set them from the start as it is much harder to introduce them later on. Some things you may like to consider are:

Live-out help
- Lunch breaks and tea breaks.
- Agreeing flexible hours/overtime.
- Food usage/particular requirements.
- Taking personal calls at work.
- Managing petty cash.
- Confidentiality.
- Car usage.
- Punctuality/reliability.

Live-in help
- Eating together/separately in the evening.
- Internet and computer access.
- Phone usage and times.
- Bath/shower times if limited hot water.
- Coming-in times in the evening.
- Boyfriend and visitor times.
- Smoking and drinking.
- Car usage out of work hours.

> *'Set boundaries from the beginning or live to regret it.'*

People can feel particularly awkward setting boundaries for au pairs, who in essence, are guests in their home. However, relevant boundaries mean fewer issues and awkward situations.

> *'It all went wrong when I was on maternity leave. There was a lack of boundaries and as I played with the children she resented having to do the chores. She had more flexibility when I was at work – she didn't like me being at home.'*

For example, you may feel that you should invite your au pair to eat and sit with you every evening, but not really want her to. In fact she may prefer to spend time on the internet or the phone and most certainly watching different TV programmes from you. Don't be afraid to say that you are old and boring and she would probably prefer to amuse herself in the evenings, or that you don't feel you see your partner enough and would prefer to spend the evenings alone together.

It is also important to set the boundaries for your communication. You need to get on well with your nanny, maternity nurse or au pair and get to know her, but be careful not to become too friendly, as this makes the professional relationship harder to manage. Keep in mind what your limits are, as to what information you will share and what you would rather not. If she goes beyond these, you can pleasantly move on from the topic and she will soon understand the limits. This can all be done in a very friendly way. You need to balance this with the need to be sympathetic to any big problems that she may be having. You can still give an au pair who is feeling homesick lots of time and attention without blurring the boundaries.

> *'I welcomed my first nanny in as a friend and it was a disaster. With the second I was a bit more stand offish, more the boss and it was so much better.'*

3 Communicate

Communication is at the heart of working well with your childcarer. If a friend or relative is your childcarer you want to ensure you do not jeopardise your friendship or family relationship. If your au pair has poor English you need to think how to communicate effectively. Whoever your childcarer is and however much you see her during the day, you need to agree how you would both prefer to communicate to ensure you work well together. Issues you may consider are:

- When and how you will tell each other key information, for example, at the beginning and end of the working day.

> *'She is lovely but just talks so much I can't get things done! I now make the time to talk once a week. If I can't do it one day I will make a time to talk to her the next day – it takes half an hour once a week but is well worth it. It is something she needs.'*

- How to communicate when you are out – text, calls or radio silence.
- How you could both be prepared to use compromise and flexibility to keep things working well.
- How you will both deal with issues or niggles.

> *'I don't want to put her down, so I let it ride to see if she picks up the problem and deals with it, but then she accepts that it is okay and then how do I tell her it is wrong?'*

It is vital that you keep communication going on a day-to-day basis. Discuss the children, the week ahead and any difficulties or successes she has had. As you know, running a home and battling with small children can wear you down. Do take note of her achievements or tough days. Thank and sympathise accordingly – it will mean an awful lot. All the answers for making it work lie between the two of you – you have to be able to find them.

> *'Make time to listen and communicate, make them feel valued as a person.'*

As most au pairs and mother's helps are unqualified and some also have little or no experience, they can need more support and guidance than other forms of childcare. However, communicating with them from the beginning should result in them doing things exactly as you want. As their experience increases, so should your confidence in their abilities, meaning that you can ask them to do additional tasks.

In the case of a nanny share, you need to communicate with your nanny and with the other family involved. You need to be clear about what you need, while remaining open to new ideas. The best shares survive on good communication and compromise between like-minded families.

Reviews

Part of communicating well should involve regular reviews. You are probably far less likely to carry these out with a friend or relative – it may sound too work-like – but they are essential. You are reviewing how the arrangement is working and giving an opportunity to discuss concerns and worries and to exchange ideas that you might not have the time to mention during a busy week.

> *'The reviews help, as you feel you know where you stand. In fact, everyone knows where they stand and you know if they are happy with you.' – Clare, nanny to three children*

Before your new childcarer starts, it is always a good idea to think how you will manage the reviews. All too often people intend to carry these out but either lack the confidence to do it, worry about giving and receiving negative comments, or simply don't find the time to fit them in. Asking every now and again if everything is okay is not a substitute for a review and all you will usually get is a polite 'yes'.

Reviews can take the form of a formal meeting but usually work best as an informal chat. Ensure you carry them out regularly, be it once a month or once every six months. The more you do them, the easier they will become. If you feel apprehensive, start them off as a relaxed 10–15 minute chat over a cup of coffee. You might like to arrange to go out for lunch together.

'Every three months my husband comes home early and puts the children to bed and she and I go round the corner to the wine bar, to have a catch up.'

If employing a maternity nurse you may like to have a 10-minute chat and review every week or two.

At the review, you should discuss how the arrangement is working for her and if she would like to change anything. Ensure you praise all the good stuff and her hard work. Discuss how it is working for you and if you would like to change anything. Further discuss the children, their development and any changes that need to be made. Where necessary, discuss and come up with ideas to help with any developmental or behavioural issues. You need to work as a team and it is nice for both of you to feel you have a shoulder to lean on. Having had a review, it is essential that you act on what you agree.

'I didn't have the confidence to do monthly meetings. I made it into a bit of a thing but I shouldn't have. I should have just sat down and had lunch with her. I would have built up my confidence and she would have built up hers.'

4 Ensure your child is happy

Your childcare arrangement will only ever work well if your child is happy. You know your child better than anyone else, and need to assess how settled he or she is. However, do remember that children generally plump for a parent over anyone else and may pull every stunt in the book to get their preference. If you are concerned:

- Come home unannounced and assess whether things are running smoothly. Assess whether the job is being done properly and how your child is when you are not there or expected.
- Note if your child is behaving differently – more withdrawn or aggressive. Are there any unexplained bruises or cuts? Do they make any comments that worry you?
- Note whether your childcarer is aware of your child's feelings.
- Talk to her and judge her response. Is she constructive in making suggestions about why your child is reacting in this way? Does she come up with some good ideas to rectify the situation and put them into action? Is there anything that is bothering her that means she is not putting her all into the job?

If you do have concerns, it is vitally important that you talk to your child (if possible) and the childcarer and listen to what they both say –

however, the final decision will rest with you. Your child may just need a bit more time to get settled. If things don't improve, a different childcarer or a different type of childcare might need to be considered.

> *'You end up losing your cool and doing something extreme. When my nanny did not correct my 2-year-old for throwing food on the floor after three days, I picked up the whole highchair with child in it and put her in the corner facing the wall. I told her sternly that if she did it again the same thing would happen. She stopped doing it but I realised I had ended up taking my anger at the nanny out on the child. Sometimes it is like a dysfunctional marriage – you end up talking to the nanny through the child.'*

If your au pair or mother's help is inexperienced or lacking in confidence, you may need to be particularly vigilant. Some children react to this situation by refusing to do what they are told and even telling the carer what to do. This results in a lack of boundaries for the child, a rude and stubborn charge for the carer and a very unhappy household for you!

> *'I kept reminding her that my son was 3 and she was 23 and had to be in charge. In the end I got her to practise telling off our giant teddy bear, and that seemed to increase her confidence.'*

5 Don't take them for granted

As many a mother and wife knows, nothing is worse than being taken for granted. This is how your childcarer will feel if you do not stick to what you have agreed in terms of communication, ground rules and, very importantly, handover times. It is easy to fall back into old habits, particularly if we are busy or stressed but if you break your side of the agreement, your childcarer is sure to lose motivation. You must always treat your childcarer with respect and always be aware of how you are reacting towards her, and why. Always thank her for her hard work and also find other ways to show your appreciation.

> *'It is really nice when they surprise you and let you finish work a couple of hours early. It doesn't have to be too often, just now and again.' – Zoe, nanny to four children*

You are much more likely to be late picking a child up from a friend or relative than any other form of childcare. How they must dread the phone ringing and hearing 'Something has come up. Do you mind keeping them for a couple more hours, and bathing them while you are at it. Thanks!' Bear in mind, too, that we are less likely to thank those who are closest to us.

*'If you say you are going to be home by 4pm, make sure you are; just
because they are family don't take liberties.'*

A nanny share requires you to be particularly flexible and willing to
compromise as by nature this arrangement can be more complicated.
Remember to take neither your nanny nor the other family involved for
granted. Also consider that your nanny is trying to please two bosses so
listen to any suggestions and make it a three-way conversation.

*'It is wonderful if you can have them for a long time. We have had
our au pair for two years and she does everything how I would do it.
At times you do have to point out what they are doing wrong and you
always have to make sure they have everything they need.'*

Solving problems

You may feel awkward or silly bringing up an issue, but not dealing with it
will only make you, and potentially your child, unhappy. Any good
childcarer would rather you raised an issue, so it can be dealt with. If other
children are also present, at a nursery or childminder's, for example, it is
important that similar issues do not affect others.

*'I hate confrontation but push myself to do it, as I think it is so
important to sort problems out with your nursery.'*

Unless there is a serious breach of safety you can often sort out a
problem in a non-confrontational way:

- Take time to think about it, rather than reacting immediately.
- In a nursery, pre-school or out-of-school club, always try to discuss it with
  your child's key worker, teacher or play worker rather than going over his or
  her head.

*'Don't worry too much about it or let it fester, just please come and
talk to us.' – Ann, pre-school supervisor*

- Think about how everyone is feeling or acting and use this as the basis for
  tackling the problem. See the tables on pages 200–203 for examples of how
  to do this.
- Choose a good time to bring the issue up, or schedule in a five-minute
  discussion.

It is hard to broach an issue with any childcarer. Some subjects will be
harder to broach with a friend or relative and some easier. However, keep
in mind that tempers may rise and affront be taken more easily when
dealing with a friend or relative.

Take time to think about how to raise issues or problems, but aim to resolve things sooner rather than later. In the case of in-home care, don't bite your childcarer's head off if you come home and things are not as you would like. This will not get anyone anywhere, apart from your child off to another form of childcare. Nipping things in the bud will avoid tension and resentment build-up, and also ensure things are done as you would like. You don't want to give your childcarer mixed messages by being 'nice on top but cross underneath'.

> *'I have learnt that it is better to say something than let it eat away at you.'*

Also find out how your childcarer would like to bring issues up with you. This shows that you know some problems are likely to come up and that you are ready to listen and solve them. This will also stop something minor developing into a bigger problem. You may be surprised at how hard a childcarer finds it to talk about something that is going wrong.

> *'I know I should say something if a problem comes up; I have definitely got braver over the years!' – Shelley, childminder*

The following tables show how specific problems in particular childcare setting can be approached from a number of angles:

Your child is being bitten by another child at nursery	
You	'I understand that Freddie has been bitten by Tom again. It is obviously upsetting for him but I also don't want Freddie to start biting too. I know you have tried various things, but can you think of anything else you could do to stop Tom doing it?'
Your child	'Freddie used to look forward to coming to nursery, but now that Tom keeps biting him, he is more reluctant. The whole thing is very upsetting for him. Can you think of anything you could do to stop Tom biting him?'
Your nursery	'I know it is hard for you to monitor all the children all the time, but I understand that Tom has been biting Freddie again. It must cause quite a commotion for everyone each time it happens. I know you have tried various things but can you think of anything else you could do to stop Tom doing it?'

> *'Think before you speak. Don't be impulsive – you will either be too harsh or too generous and regret it.'*

Your child has a new teacher at pre-school and seems to react to this	
You	'Poppy seemed to be so settled but since the change in teachers she does not seem to want to come to school each morning. What do you think could be done to help her settle? I find it very stressful seeing her so upset in the morning and worry about her all day.'
Your child	'Poppy is working herself up into quite a state each morning before school. It seems to be as a result of the change in teachers. Can you think of anything else it could be or anything we could do to make her life a bit happier?'
Your preschool	'I know it must be difficult when there is a change in staff and the teacher has to get to know the children. I wondered if we could talk about how to get Poppy to settle back in. I am sure it would make your life easier if she was a bit happier about coming to school.'

Your child does not seem to be eating enough at the childminder's	
You	'I am sorry, but I always really fret if Emily doesn't eat. Can you think of anything that you or I could do to make her eat a better lunch with you? It would make me worry less.'
Your child	'Emily is always quite tired in the evening and not that keen to eat. I try to get her to eat a good lunch, which she doesn't always seem to do when with you. Can you think of anything you or I could do to make her eat a better lunch with you?'
Your childminder	'I know it must be a battle for you to try to get Emily to eat her lunch. Can you think of anything that you or I could do to make her eat better with you? I am sure it would make your life easier, and she would be a happier child for you in the afternoon.'

'When I was cross I used to bang around and use actions instead of words. It was a bad and negative form of communication, which I now realise.'

Your child seems really hyped up when he leaves an after-school club	
You	'Max is very over excited when he leaves after-school club, which is a bit out of character. He clearly enjoys it but when we leave he races out and is so hyped up he won't listen to me. It may sound a bit neurotic, but I am terrified one day he may race out into the road as we leave. Can you think why this is happening and what could be done to calm him down a bit?'
Your child	'Max is always very over excited when he leaves after-school club. It seems to take him quite a bit of time to wind down when we get home. Consequently our evenings run later and he gets to bed late, meaning he is tired in the mornings. As you can imagine, he is pretty exhausted by the end of the week. Can you think why this is happening and what could be done to calm him down a bit?'
Your out-of-school club	'I am sure you have noticed that Max is rather hyped up when he leaves after-school club. I don't know if this is the case with other children and if they are all revving each other up. It must be a fairly hectic session for you all. Can you think why this is happening and what could be done to calm him down a bit? I am sure it would make your afternoons a lot more pleasant!'

You feel your children are not getting enough fresh air when with your friend or relative	
You	'I read something that says children get fewer colds in winter if they have fresh air every day. It keeps their immune system healthy. Do you think you can ensure this happens even if it is a quick walk to the post office or 10 minutes at the play park? I will feel so much happier and the children should be ill less often.'
Your children	'They have so much energy and can start to fight if they don't burn it off. Do you think you can ensure they get out in the afternoons, then Fred will stop beating up poor Tom!'
Your friend or relative	'I know you can find the children quite difficult towards the end of the day. I find that if they have some fresh air in the afternoon, they then come in and play quietly until tea time. Do you want to try it and see if it makes the afternoons calmer for you?'

You must always put yourself in their shoes and it must be give and take.'

Your nanny is consistently late for work	
You	'I know I can sometimes run late too. From now on shall we both try hard to stick to our agreed timings?'
Your children	'The chaos and stress of everyone running late in the mornings is quite upsetting for the children. I think we all need to be organised and more on time. Is that okay with you?'
Your nanny	'Poor you. I know it is a nightmare getting here in the rush hour and it is awful to arrive at work all flustered. What do you think would help you to get here on time?'

'Acknowledge that your nanny is human and can't always be on top form, they will have bad days too.' – Zoe, nanny to four children

The kitchen table is not being wiped properly after meals by the au pair or mother's help	
You	'I know I am probably being neurotic – I think it is those disinfectant ads on TV that show the germs in a kitchen! But could you always ensure the table is clean after the children have eaten?'
Your children	'I always make the children wipe the table after they have been painting or using play dough. I have been thinking that you and I must practise what we preach and make sure we do the same after mealtimes!'
Your au pair or mother's help	'Could you always ensure the table is clean after the children have eaten? I noticed they are rubbing their hands in what is left on it and then they wipe it on their clothes. It will help to keep the washing pile down, and I know the washing is the bit of the job you enjoy the least.'

If things are not resolved

In a nursery, pre-school or out-of-school club, if you feel an issue has not been resolved by talking to those immediately involved, you should then take things up with the supervisor in charge of your key worker, teacher or play worker or, depending on the severity of the problem, with the manager. Be careful not to jump too far up the hierarchy as people will resent this. If the nursery or pre-school is attached to a school, the head teacher will be your final port of call. Try to resolve it amicably and constructively. If you still feel you need to take things further you should find out about the complaints policy and follow this accordingly.

If things get heated

If things reach a crisis point you need to sort out a solution as soon as possible. This stage may well signal the end of the childcare arrangement. Here are some pointers:

- Never lose your temper. Don't say things you may regret as this can ruin not only the childcare arrangement but damage your relationship if your childcarer is also a friend or relative.
- Agree a time to talk it through, if possible without children present. This gives everyone a chance to reflect.
- If you have a contract, check what has been agreed about termination. A nanny or au pair contract may include a clause about warnings.
- If appropriate, ask the childcarer to talk first. Ensure you do not interrupt or get defensive, but do ask additional questions for clarity and when she has finished confirm what you have heard. Then outline your view of the situation. Limit what you are saying to the issue in hand, without bringing in additional gripes unless they are relevant and build on your point.
- Talk candidly about how the situation can be solved, offer solutions and ask the childcarer to offer thoughts and ideas. Hopefully you will clear the air and find a suitable solution, becoming a stronger team.
- If you are unable to find a solution, you may have to look at terminating the contract. This could be with immediate effect and you may have to find some emergency childcare. If possible, agree that there are no bad feelings on either side – you tried and it did not work out.

> *'If it is ending badly you just have to end it immediately. I limped on once with someone for a couple of months, while we looked for someone new, and it was just dreadful.'*

- Always, always be fair, honest and, whenever possible, friendly and compassionate. Childminders, in particular, are likely to live close to you and you do not want local gossip or to find that no other childminder will take your child on.
- In the case of a friend or relative, do not let any disagreements affect your relationship – be prepared to swallow your pride for the sake of harmony!
- If you reach this point with an au pair, do remember it can be very stressful to be in such a position so far from home when you are relatively young.
- If things do not work out, an au pair will need to make arrangements to find somewhere else to live or to leave the country; ensure you give her enough time and support to do this.

Part 5

Reference Section

Outline of Childcare Qualifications

There are dozens of childcare qualifications available in the UK, but what follows are the main recognised courses that are available. These do change in terms of names and content over time (source: Bestbear.co.uk).

CACHE (Council for Awards in Children's Care and Education)
This is a specialist body that develops courses and qualifications in childcare. Courses include:

- **CACHE Level 2, Certificate in Childcare and Education (CCE)** or **Certificate in Children's Care Learning and Development (CCCLD)** These qualify people to be childcare assistants.

- **CACHE Level 3, Diploma in Childcare and Education (DCE)** (previously known as NNEB)

    Equivalent to two A Levels, this covers health, safety, nutrition and educational play – 40 per cent of the course is spent on placements in homes, nurseries, hospitals and junior schools. This qualifies people to work with children in an unsupervised role such as a childminder, nursery nurse or nanny.

- **CACHE Level 3 Certificate in Childminding Practice (CCP)** This is developed with the National Childminding Association (NCMA).

    For more information or to verify a CACHE qualification call 0845 347 2123 or go to cache.org.uk.

BTEC (Business and Technology Education Council)
These courses have a slightly more academic emphasis than others:

- **BTEC First Diploma in Children's Care, Learning and Development** (equivalent of four GCSEs)

- **BTEC National Award in Children's Care, Learning and Development** (equivalent of 1 A Level)

- **BTEC National Certificate in Children's Care, Learning and Development** (equivalent of 2 A Levels)

- **BTEC National Diploma in Children's Care, Learning and Development** (equivalent of 3 A Levels)

- **BTEC Higher National Certificate (HNC)** or **Diploma (HND) in Advanced Practice in Work with Children and Families**

  For further information call 0844 576 0026 or go to edexcel.org.uk.

NVQs and SVQs

NVQs (National Vocational Qualifications) and SVQs (Scottish Vocational Qualifications) are based on practical experience in the workplace. Courses include:

- **Children's Care, Learning and Development – Level 2**
  This is obtained by a childcare worker in a supervised role, for example, nursery assistant, playgroup worker, childminder, experienced but untrained nanny.

- **Children's Care, Learning and Development – Level 3**
  For more experienced childcarers. This could be considered the equivalent of a DCE (see CACHE on previous page).

- **Children's Care, Learning and Development – Level 4**
  For childcarers in management positions.

City and Guilds NVQs and SVQs

These include **Children's Care, Learning and Development to Level 2, 3 and 4** (SVQ Level 2 and 3 only). They are similar in content to the CACHE courses, but can give a broader base in childcare including the care of sick or disabled children. To check a candidate's qualifications call 0121 503 8993 or for more information go to city-and-guilds.co.uk.

Montessori

The Montessori Centre International offers an internationally renowned qualification in the Montessori method. Montessori teachers have a minimum of a college degree and a year's student teaching under supervision. They will be qualified to work with infants, toddlers, pre-primary or elementary-level children. For more details call 0207 493 0165 or go to montessori.uk.com.

Maternity nurses

Most maternity nurse courses are intensive courses of a few days or a week, which experienced nannies or midwives use to top up their skills. The best qualifications will be accredited by a recognised awarding body such as CACHE.

Childcarer Characteristics

- Relaxed and friendly
- Keen to learn
- Safety conscious
- Good with routine and structure
- Able to think on his or her feet
- Able to think ahead/use initiative
- Enthusiastic/confident/outgoing
- Flexible/adaptable
- Quiet and reserved
- Compassionate
- Loving but firm/able to discipline
- Able to cook/swim/ride, etc.
- Calm/unruffled/patient
- Reliable/responsible
- Punctual/a good timekeeper
- Caring/kind/warm/loving
- Open/honest/trustworthy
- Creative and playful
- Cheerful
- Relaxed yet responsible
- Gives attention to detail
- Has a sense of humour
- Upbeat/positive/cheerful
- Can give long-term job commitment

Sample Nanny Job Description

Nanny duties and responsibilities

- To care for Fintan (3), Thea (2) and Lorne (6 months), ensuring they are safe, healthy, happy and well looked after.
- To prepare balanced and healthy meals for all three children, compiling a shopping list once a week.
- To help wean Lorne on to solids, ensuring this is done at the right pace and only with fresh foods.
- To wash, iron and put away all the children's clothes. Once every three months, to sort through drawers and collect all the clothes the children have grown out of.
- To keep tidy and maintain the children's bedrooms and playroom. To encourage the children to tidy their bedrooms and playroom.
- To keep the toys in the playroom in an ordered fashion so they are easily accessible.
- To plan a varied number of outings and activities for the children, using your initiative and enthusiasm, with appropriate developmental opportunities.
- To assist Fin and Thea in learning numbers and letters in a fun and easy-going way (and only if they are interested and enjoying it!).
- To ensure (unless the weather is totally dreadful) the children get fresh air every day. If walking in the fields, when possible, to take the dog with you on a lead.
- To deliver and collect Fin and Thea to and from nursery school as necessary.
- To plan the week ahead with me to ensure you and the children are kept happy and busy.
- To be flexible in your working hours, generally starting early (7am) two mornings a week and working late (7.30pm or 8pm) two evenings a week. However, your hours per week will not exceed 48 unless otherwise agreed beforehand.
- To babysit six nights per month if the dates suit you.
- To accompany the family on holidays if the dates suit you.
- To suggest to me any ideas you have on doing things in a different/better way and to let me know if you are not happy with anything.
- To assist with three simple household duties: filling and emptying the dishwasher, feeding the dog if you are on duty at the appropriate time and emptying the bin as necessary.
- To enjoy your job and be happy!

Sample Nanny Ad

Marry the characteristics you would like with the skills required and other details. An example of a shorter ad is:

> Outdoor-orientated, friendly family living in a small Wiltshire village need a live-in full-time nanny to look after our 2-year-old girl and 3-year-old boy. Must have previously had sole charge of at least two children under the age of 4. Must be caring, reliable and able to use their initiative. Driving and good English essential. Car supplied with job. Non-smoker please. Contact Laura on 012345 678910 or laura@1234567.co.uk.

A longer ad gives more details of the job and your family, and can be used on a website, for example:

> We are a friendly, active family living in a small Wiltshire village, half an hour from Bristol. We are looking for a full-time, live-in nanny (55 hours a week) to look after our 2-year-old girl and 3-year-old boy. I work from home three days a week, am in London one day a week and spend Fridays with the children. Our little boy will be starting nursery three mornings a week.
>
> You must have previously had sole charge of at least two children under the age of 4. You must be cheerful, caring, reliable and able to use your initiative. You must be happy to have shared charge one day a week. Someone with a reputable childcare qualification would be preferred.
>
> Driving and good English are essential and a car is supplied. We offer a double bedroom with its own bathroom, TV, phone and broadband connection. Although small, our village is lively. There is a pub and another nanny lives in the village. Non-smoker please. Contact Laura on 012345 678910 or laura@1234567.co.uk. We look forward to hearing from you!

In-home Childcare Assessment Sheet

Name: **Contact details:**

Must have	Would be nice

- Relevant experience and qualifications:
- Approach to childcare and values:
- Did the children/I/my partner like her?
- Communication skills?
- Stable background and past?
- Commitment and enthusiasm for the job?
- Available to start:

Other good things	Concerns or worries

Sample Nanny Employment Contract

NAME AND ADDRESS OF EMPLOYER   …………………………………..
  …………………………………..
  …………………………………..
  …………………………………..

NAME AND ADDRESS OF EMPLOYEE   …………………………………..
  …………………………………..
  …………………………………..
  …………………………………..

START DATE OF EMPLOYMENT   …………………………………..

JOB TITLE   …………………………………..

PLACE OF WORK   …………………………………..

CHILDREN

NAME ………………………………........   AGE …………….

NAME ………………………………........   AGE …………….

NAME ………………………………........   AGE …………….

NAME ………………………………........   AGE …………….

DUTIES
- Taking care of the day-to-day needs of the children
- Planning activities, organising play dates and outings
- Providing educational play, arts and crafts
- Helping with homework and school projects
- Creating a safe, stimulating and loving environment
- Planning, shopping for and preparing nutritious food (incl. homemade baby food)
- Organisation and upkeep of children's toys and play areas
- Children's washing (incl. bed linen and towels) and children's ironing
- Raising any childcare-related issues with parents and working together to find a solution
- Any other tasks needed to be carried out best to serve the interests and promote the happiness of the children

REMUNERATION

The basic salary is £ .... net per week. Payable weekly/monthly on ....
The Employer is responsible for paying the Employee's tax and National
Insurance contributions.
Overtime will be paid at £ .... net per hour.
The salary will be reviewed after .... months.
The Employer will provide the Employee with a pay slip each month, a P60 at
the end of each tax year and P45 at the end of the employment.

HOURS OF WORK

Monday .... am to .... pm
Tuesday .... am to .... pm
Wednesday .... am to .... pm
Thursday .... am to .... pm
Friday .... am to .... pm
Saturday .... am to .... pm
Sunday .... am to .... pm

(Live in)
Babysitting .... nights per week included in the Employee's salary.
(Live out)
Babysitting .... nights per week paid at a rate of .... net per hour.

EXPENSES

Expenses incurred during the working day to include:
• travel/fuel
• outings and activities
• soft drinks, tea and coffee, etc.
• grocery shopping for food for the Employee and children
• other purchases on behalf of the children with prior agreement of the
  Employer.

The Employer will provide £ .... per week for such expenses. Any weekly
costs above this amount must be previously agreed with the Employer.
The Employee will keep a record of such expenses (cash book).

ACCOMMODATION

The following level of accommodation will be provided:
• private bedroom
• private/shared bathroom
• private sitting room
• private kitchen
The Employee's right to occupy this accommodation will cease on termination
of employment, howsoever arising. The Employee shall immediately vacate
the Employer's home.

USE OF CAR
- The Employee will have use of a car on duty.
- The Employee will have sole use of a car on and off duty.
- The Employer is responsible for insurance and maintenance of the car.
- The Employer will pay for fuel during the working day.
- The Employee will pay for fuel during private use.
- The Employer has the right to withdraw the benefit of the use of the car if changes in the Employee's circumstances occur that could invalidate or affect the insurance policy.
- Fuel costs will be reimbursed at the rate recommended by the AA if the Employee uses their own car.

HOLIDAYS
- The holiday year will run from .... to ....
- .... days paid holiday, plus bank holidays and other public holidays.
- .... days to be the Employee's choice (minimum one month's notice to be given).
- Compensation for untaken holidays is at the discretion of the Employer.
- Holidays may only be carried into the next year at the discretion of the Employer.

SICKNESS
The Employer will pay Standard Sick Pay (SSP) according to current legislation. Any additional sick pay is at the discretion of the Employer.

PENSION
The Employer will/will not provide pension entitlements.
(Note: If five or more individuals are employed in the house it will be necessary for the Employer to provide access to a stakeholder pension.)

DISCIPLINARY PROCEDURE
Disciplinary action may occur for the following reasons but not limited to: incompetence, unsatisfactory conduct, unreliability, breech of confidentiality, failure to comply with instruction/procedure.

First: oral warning
Second: written warning
Third: dismissal – 3-STEP DISMISSAL PROCESS must be followed

3-STEP DISMISSAL PROCESS
1 Letter to Employee confirming time for Employer, Employee and Employee's representative (or friend) to attend a meeting (48 hours' notice must be given).
2 Meeting to discuss reasons for dismissal.
3 Letter confirming dismissal and giving the Employee the right to appeal.

IMMEDIATE SUSPENSION shall occur for the following reasons but not limited to: child abuse, serious misconduct, serious breach of confidentiality, dishonesty, illegal drug taking, drunkenness, theft, violent or threatening behaviour.

If the Employee is suspended, pending dismissal, the 3-STEP DISMISSAL PROCESS must still be followed.

TERMINATION OF EMPLOYMENT
- First four weeks of employment .... days/weeks written notice by either party.
- After four weeks of employment .... weeks/months' written notice by either party.
- (Statutory minimum notice period – one week's notice per year of service. Maximum 12 weeks).

On termination of employment for whatever reason, the Employee must immediately return to the Employer any property relating to the Employer and Employer's residence.

CONFIDENTIALITY
The Employee must keep the affairs of the Employer's household and business strictly confidential both during and following employment.

This includes written or oral statements and comments to any person or any member of the press or broadcasting media.

The above restrictions do not affect any other duties of trust, confidence or good faith that may be implied into this contract of employment.

GOVERNING LAW
This contract shall be governed by English Law and you must submit to the jurisdiction of the English courts to determine any matter arising in connection with this contract.

Your signature below will constitute your agreement to the terms set out above.

EMPLOYER'S SIGNATURE   EMPLOYEE'S SIGNATURE

DATE ....   DATE ....

Please note that whilst every effort is made to ensure the accuracy of the information given, this contract offers an outline of the law as it applies in the most common cases only. It should not be relied on as a complete statement of the law and anyone considering taking action should consult a suitably qualified lawyer or employment law expert.

Useful Sources of Information

Association of Nanny Agencies (ANA)
anauk.org

Best Bear Childcare
Childcare advice and search site
08707 201277
bestbear.co.uk

Border and Immigration Agency
bia.homeoffice.gov.uk

British Au Pair Agencies Association (BAPAA)
07946 149 916
info@bapaa.org.uk
bapaa.org.uk

BTEC (Business and Technology Education Council)
Provides childcare training and courses
0844 576 0026
edexcel.org.uk

Care and Social Services Inspectorate Wales
01443 848450
cssiw@wales.gsi.gov.uk
cssiw.org.uk

Care to Learn
Information and help with accessing childcare while you learn
0845 600 2809
dfes.gov.uk/caretolearn

Childcare Vouchers
hmrc.gov.uk/childcare

Childcarelink
National and local childcare information
0800 2346 346 (freephone)
childlink.gov.uk

City and Guilds
Provides childcare training and courses
0121 503 8993
city-and-guilds.co.uk

Contact a Family
A UK-wide charity providing support, advice and information for families with disabled children
020 7608 8700
0808 808 3555 (helpline), 0808 808 3556 (textphone) – freephone for parents and families (Monday–Friday, 10am–4pm and Monday 5.30–7.30pm)
info@cafamily.org.uk
cafamily.org.uk

Council for Awards in Children's Care and Education (CACHE)
Provides childcare training and courses
0845 347 2123
cache.org.uk

Criminal Records Bureau
crb.gov.uk

Daycare Trust
Provides free information on a range of childcare issues including childcare options, where to find childcare and how to find help with childcare costs
020 7840 3350 (helpline) Monday, Wednesday and Friday 10am–5pm
info@daycaretrust.org.uk
daycaretrust.org.uk

Department for Children, Schools and Families
Public enquiry unit
0870 0002288 (to order a copy of the SEN Code of Practice, call 0845 6022260)
info@dcsf.gsi.gov.uk
dfes.gov.uk

**Department of Education for
Northern Ireland**
028 9127 9279
mail@deni.gov.uk
deni.gov.uk

**Department of Health, Social Services
and Public Safety, Northern Ireland**
028 90520500
webmaster@dhsspsni.gov.uk
dhsspsni.gov.uk

Directgov
Government information site
direct.gov.uk

Employers for Childcare
Childcare advice and information
helpline, Northern Ireland
0800 028 3008 (freephone/text)
employersforchildcare.org

Every Child Matters
everychildmatters.gov.uk

Gingerbread
Offers support and advice to lone
parent families
0800 018 5026 (Monday–Friday 9am–
5pm, Wednesday 9am–8pm)
gingerbread.org.uk

Grandparents' Association
Offers relevant support and advice to
grandparents
0845 434 9585 (advice line)
grandparents-association.org.uk

**The Independent Schools Council
(ISC)**
Provides information about private
nursery schools in your area
0845 7246657
isc.co.uk

Inland Revenue
hmrc.gov.uk

LCF Clubs
After-school clubs offering French and
Spanish
01489 786473
admin@lcfclubs.com
lcfclubs.com

Learning and Teaching Scotland
08700 100 297 (customer services)
enquiries@LTScotland.org.uk
ltscotland.org.uk

Montessori Centre International
Provides training and courses in the
Montessori method
020 7493 0165
montessori.uk.com

Montessori Education UK
A guide to Montessori education and a
list of accredited schools
montessorieducationuk.org

NannyCheck
Provides background checks for nannies
and au pairs
020 8123 7212
info@nanny-check.co.uk
nanny-check.co.uk

NannySuccess.com
Helps you find and manage your nanny,
au pair or housekeeper
01285 810410
info@nannysuccess.com
nannysuccess.com

Nannytax
Provides a payroll support service for
parents employing in-home childcare
0845 226 2203
mailbox@nannytax.co.uk
nannytax.co.uk

**National Association of Children's
Information Services (NACIS)**
A registered charity that supports, links
and promotes children's information
services
nacis.org.uk

National Childbirth Trust (NCT)
Offers support and advice for expectant and new parents
0870 444 8707 (9am–5pm Monday–Thursday, 9am–4pm Friday)
nct.org.uk

National Childminding Association of England and Wales (NCMA)
0800 169 4486 (freephone)
10am–4pm Monday to Friday
ncma.org.uk

National Day Nurseries Association (NDNA)
01484 407070
ndna.org.uk

Netmums
A network site for mums (and dads), offering information on a national and local level
netmums.com

Northern Ireland Childminding Association
028 9181 1015
nicma.org

Ofsted
For information on the Childcare Register, both Compulsory and Voluntary
08456 404040
ofsted.gov.uk

Parentlineplus
A national charity that works for, and with, parents
0808 800 2222 (freephone)
parentlineplus.org.uk

The PreSchool Directory
Lists day nurseries, nursery schools and pre-schools in your area
preschooldirectory.co.uk

Royal Society for the Prevention of Accidents
0121 248 2000
help@rospa.com
rospa.com

Safe and Sound
Child safety and first aid courses
020 8449 8722
safe-and-sound.org.uk

Scottish Childcare Information
scottishchildcare.gov.uk

Scottish Childminding Association
01786 445377
childminding.org

Scottish Commission for the Regulation of Care (SCRC)
0845 603 0890
carecommission.com

SNAP Childcare (Special Needs Agency Partnership)
An agency specialising in finding in-home childcare for children with special needs
020 7729 2200
info@snapchildcare.co.uk
snapchildcare.co.uk

Sure Start
surestart.gov.uk

Tax Credits and Working Tax Credits
0845 300 3900
http://taxcredits.direct.gov.uk

Wales Pre-School Playgroups Association
01686 624573
walesppa.org

Way2paye
Provides a payroll support service for parents employing in-home childcare
01604 743346
way2paye.co.uk

Welsh Assembly Government site
accac.org.uk
new.wales.gov.uk

Working Families
020 7253 7243
workingfamilies.org.uk

Sites for searching or placing job postings for nannies, nanny shares and au pairs
aupair-world.net
greataupair.com
greatcare.co.uk
gumtree.com
nannyjob.co.uk
nannyselect.co.uk

Sites for searching for potential nanny shares
nannyshare.co.uk
thenannysharers.co.uk

Magazines in which you might place an ad
The Lady
lady.co.uk

Nursery World
0208 267 4674
nurseryworldjobs.co.uk

Horse and Hound
(for a nanny/groom)
horseandhound.co.uk

Index